Admission to Communion:

The Approaches of the Late Medievals and the Reformers

Mark Dalby

Sometime Archdeacon of Rochdale

Abbreviations

CR *Corpus Reformatorum*, Brunswick 1834–1900, Leipzig 1904ff.
Fisher BMW J. D. C. Fisher, *Christian Initiation: Baptism in the Medieval West* (SPCK, London, 1965)
Fisher RP J. D. C. Fisher, *Christian Initiation: The Reformation Period* (SPCK, London, 1970).
LW *Luther's Works*, eds J. Pelikan and H. T. Lehmann, 56 vols (Concordia Publishing House, Philadelphia and St Louis, 1955ff.).
Mansi J. D. Mansi, *Sacrorum Conciliorum Nova et Amplissima Collectio*. 53 vols (Welter, Paris and Leipzig 1903–27).
Ollard S. L. Ollard, 'Confirmation in the Anglican Communion' in *Confirmation or the Laying on of Hands*, by Various Writers, vol.1, (SPCK, London, 1926).
PC F. M. Powicke and C. R. Cheney, *Councils and Synods with other Documents relating to the English Church*, Vol. II (Clarendon, Oxford 1964).
PL *Patrologia Latina*, ed. J. P. Migne, 221 vols (Paris, 1844–64).
PS Parker Society (Cambridge, 1841–55).
WA *D. Martin Luthers Werke, Kritische Gesamtausgabe*, Weimar, 1883ff.
Biblical quotations are usually from the Revised Version.

The cover picture is from Richard Day's *Book of Christian Prayers*, 1578.
First published May 2013
© Mark Dalby 2013
ISSN: 0951-2667
ISBN: 978-1-84825-324-7

Contents

Mark Dalby: A Tribute		4
Introduction		5

A The Later Middle Ages
   1 Confirmation   6
   2 Instruction, Confession and Age   14
   3 Summary   17

B The Continental Reformation
   4 The Reformers   19
   5 The Roman Response   34

C The Church of England
   6 The Henrician Reformation   39
   7 The Edwardine Reformation   41
   8 The Elizabethan Settlement   60

D Forbidden categories
   9 Those Lacking Charity   66
   10 Strangers   67
   11 Schismatics   68

E The Discipline
   12 The Minister's Power to Repel   70

The Venerable Dr Mark Dalby (1938-2013)

For the past 10 years Mark Dalby's ambition was to complete his trilogy on infant admission to Communion. In this series of Joint Liturgical Studies he had produced work on the period from the New Testament to the Reformation in 2003 (JLS/56) and on the situation post-Reformation to the present day in 2009. (JLS/67) What was missing was a more definitive and detailed study covering the late medieval church and the reformers. Mark faithfully produced his text, but then sadly never saw it in this, its final format; he died on 11 February 2013.

His Joint Liturgical Study was one of three pieces of writing which he completed in what was to prove to be his last months.

His contribution to liturgical study had a degree of precociousness about it. He produced *Open Communion in the Church of England* while still an Oxford undergrad. Published by the Church Society, this advocated a policy of openness and hospitality which would have found few supporters among main-stream Anglicans at that time. In fact it foreshadowed his later work of which this present study is the fulfilment.

After a notable career, including time as a Selection Secretary, membership of the Liturgical Commission, and serving as Archdeacon of Rochdale in Manchester diocese, he took as his 'retirement' post the chaplaincy of the Beauchamp Community at Newlands, Malvern. This Trollopian-cum-Brideshead establishment stimulated a further interest, reflected in his JLS/41: *Anglican Missals and their Canons*. This traced the development among Prayer Book Catholics (among whom he would have numbered himself) of a desire for a richer eucharistic rite. It also chimed with the early aspirations of the Alcuin Club of which he was a trustee for a number of years.

His *Who's Who* entry lists 'travel' as the first of his 'recreations'. His other last publications were a history of the Beauchamp Community and an autobiographical travelogue, *Sixty Years of Travelling*, describing his visits to 'every country in Europe and the Med'. Then, a tantalizing and enigmatic postscript mentions places which would have deserved a revisit: 'Orporto and the Douro in Portugal, and I ought to have gone back to Belgium which I've virtually forgotten. But'

Donald Gray
Chairman of the Alcuin Club

1

Introduction

In two previous studies I have dealt with infant communion which was widely practised in the West till the thirteenth century and is currently being revived in some quarters. When the practice ceased, however, admission to communion became more a matter of ecclesiastical discipline than of Christian initiation, and the distinction between first communion and subsequent communions became blurred at times. The present study deals with admission to communion in general and first communion in particular. It begins with the background to Archbishop Peckham's famous decree of 1281 requiring confirmation before communion and concludes with the publication of the first set of Elizabethan canons in 1571. What followed thereafter is interesting but must wait for a while.

A

The Later Middle Ages

1 Confirmation

The mass was at the heart of medieval religion.[1] It was celebrated not only on Sundays and holy days, but in many places every day and sometimes many times a day. But there was a clear distinction between the offering of the mass by the priest and the receiving of communion by the laity, which was required only at Easter. Although a few communicated more frequently, the communion of the people was so rare that the form for its administration was a mere appendix to the liturgy of the mass; it did not appear in the main text. But the rarity of lay reception did not mean that it was unimportant. It was normally deemed necessary for salvation and, in order to be eligible for it, people had first to be confirmed (at least, in normal circumstances, in England), instructed and absolved after private confession.

As against instruction and confession, confirmation was a 'one-off' rite. It had an importance of its own, and, even when required before communion, it was not a ceremony of admission to communion, and it was not administered in close connection with first communion.

The so-called Canons of Edgar, c.1005–08, had laid down that 'each child is to be baptized within seven days, and that no one is to remain too long unconfirmed',[2] but some now thought that a rite of strengthening

---

[1] Cf. G. J. Cuming, *A History of Anglican Liturgy* (Macmillan, New York, 1969), pp. 15–21.
[2] No. 15, in *Councils and Synods with other documents relating to the English Church* 1 AD871–1204, ed. D. Whitelock, M. Brett and C. C. L. Brooke (Clarendon, Oxford, 1981), ii.239.

was inappropriate for infants and was best deferred. Otto of Bamberg (d.1139) had to urge that confirmation 'should not be deferred till ripe age, as some think, but should be received in the heat of youth because that age is more liable to temptations',[3] but his argument against deferment by young people was also an argument in favour of deferment by infants. Robert Pullen (d.1146), however, urged that little children should be confirmed with regard to the future,[4] and this was repeated by the author of the *Sententiae Divinitatis* (c. 1145).[5] Roland Bandinelli (later Alexander III, d.1181),[6] Roland of Cremona (c.1259)[7] and Bonaventura:[8] infants received grace, strength and virtues which, though not needed now, would be needed for their spiritual warfare, when they attained years of discretion or perfect age. One writer challenged this and asserted that 'baptism is sufficient before the years of discretion',[9] but others accepted it[10] and William of Melitona added that infant confirmation had always been the Church's custom, and that it was only because of parental neglect that it was not always the case now.[11]

St Thomas defended infant confirmation briefly in his *Scriptum super*

---

[3] *Sermo ad Pomeranos* (PL 173.1358).
[4] *Sententiae* v. 22f (PL 186.847).
[5] V. 2, ed. B. Geyer, (Aschendorff, Münster, 1909), pp. 127f., '*cum venerint ad aetatem perfectam*'.
[6] *Die Sentenzen Rolands nachmals Papstes Alexander III*, ed. A. M. Gietl, (Herdersche Verlaghandlung, Freiburg in Breisgau, 1891), p. 213, '*si ad annos discretionis pervenerit*'.
[7] *Summa* in K. F. Lynch, *The Sacrament of Confirmation in the Early-Middle Scholastic Period* (Franciscan Institute, New York, 1957), p. 83f, '*cum venient ad usum liberi arbitrii*'.
[8] *Commentaria in Quatuor Libris Sententiarum* IV dist vii.3, *Opera Omnia*, ed. Collegium Bonaventurae, Quarracchi 1882–1902, iv.173, '*postmodum*', cf. also his *Codex Autographus Super IV Sententiarum*, in Lynch, *op. cit.*, p. 43.
[9] Cf. H. Weisweiler, 'Das Sakrament der Firmung in den systematischen Werken der ersten Frühscholastik' in *Scholastik* VIII (1933), p. 493.
[10] Cf. Paris Bibl. Nat. Lat. 3032, *Commentarius in IV Librum Sententiarum*, in Lynch, *op. cit.*, p. 43; Paris Bibl. Nat. Lat. 10640, *Commentarius in IV Librum Sententiarum*, in Lynch, *op. cit.*, p. 79f, and H. Weisweiler, *art. cit.*, p. 507f..
[11] *Quaestiones de Sacramentis*, in Lynch, *op .cit.*, p. 112f..

Sententiis,[12] but he developed his position in the *Summa*. Confirmation should follow as soon after baptism as possible since it was designed 'as a remedy against that weakness to which the soul is subject for some little time after birth',[13] and it should even be given to children about to die 'so that they may be perfect at the resurrection'.[14] Still accepting that confirmation was a strengthening by the Spirit, he now developed a concept of it as a spiritual growth leading to maturity and perfect age.[15] Spiritual life, he argued, had a certain conformity with bodily life, which was perfected directly by generation, corresponding to which was baptism; by growth, corresponding to which was confirmation in which 'the Holy Spirit and strength are conferred' and by nutrition, corresponding to which was the eucharist.[16] Physically it was 'growth whereby a person attains to maturity of age', and spiritually it was at confirmation that 'a man receives maturity in the life of the spirit'.[17] But the comparison was not to be pressed too far, since the soul 'is capable of spiritual birth in old age and maturity during the years of youth and childhood because the vicissitudes of bodily age do not affect the soul'.[18]

If earlier writers had stressed that confirmation equipped a child in advance with weapons needed when he attained perfect age, St Thomas now taught that spiritually confirmation actually brought him to perfect age. But the idea of spiritual growth, like that of strengthening, involved possible confusion with the eucharist, and, to the objection that 'nourishment is the cause of growth, and in consequence prior to it', St Thomas explained that normally baptism came first, then confirmation 'to bring the soul to its due fulness of strength', and then the eucharist 'to bring it

---

[12] IV dist vii.3.2, ed. M. F. Moos, (Lethielleux, Paris, 1947), iv.294.
[13] iii.65.1, ed. T. Gilby, 1974-6, 56.142f..
[14] iii.72.8, ed. Gilby, 57.212-15.
[15] Cf. N. D. Mitchell, 'Dissolution of the Rite of Christian Initiation' in A. Kavanagh et al., *Made, not Born*, (University of Notre Dame Press, Notre Dame, 1976), pp. 59-69.
[16] iii.65.1, ed. Gilby 56.140f..
[17] iii.72.1, ed. Gilby 57.188f..
[18] iii.72.8, ed. Gilby 57.212f..

to the due fulness of the end for which it is made.[19] The eucharist would give the completion of spiritual life,[20] and all the other sacraments were ordered to the eucharist as their end: baptism was designed for the receiving of it, and confirmation gave an additional perfection so that a man would not in fear abstain from it.[21] Yet, since nourishment was 'both prior to growth as its cause and subsequent to it as maintaining man', the eucharist could be placed before confirmation as well as after it.[22]

There were unresolved anomalies here. In itself confirmation was more necessary than strong faith, reason, discretion and devotion in that it brought an infant to perfect spiritual age without these. But for admission to communion these were more necessary. Where there was reasonable impediment lack of confirmation could be excused, but strong faith, reason, discretion and devotion were demanded by the very nature of the act of communion, even though a confirmed child had already attained perfect spiritual age without them.

Confirmation presented as many problems for parish priests and parents as it did for theologians. Many dioceses were large, travel was difficult, and bishops — often few in number — were frequently preoccupied with other matters. Despite the official expectation that children would be confirmed as soon after baptism as possible, in practice they frequently attained the use of reason without being confirmed. This general delaying often led to total neglect, and throughout the thirteenth century attempts were made, especially in England, to restore confirmation to what was deemed its proper place. Some councils simply reaffirmed that parents should take their children to confirmation 'as quickly as possible'.[23] Others were more precise.

---

[19] iii.65.2, ed. Gilby 56.148f..
[20] *Scriptum super Sententiis* IV dist ix.5.4, ed. Moos iv.397.
[21] *Summa Theologiae* iii.65.3, ed. Gilby 56.152f..
[22] iii.65.2, ed. Gilby 56.148f..
[23] *Synodical Statutes for an English Diocese* 1222–5, canon ix (PC ii.141).

At Canterbury I (1213–14) the maximum interval allowed between baptism and confirmation was one year.[24] At Salisbury I (1217–19)[25] and at Canterbury II (1222–28)[26] it was 5 years; at Durham (1228–36) it was 7 years,[27] at Salisbury II (1238–44) it was still 5 years,[28] but at Worcester III (1240)[29] and Chichester I (1245–52)[30] it reverted to 1 year. For a time a happy medium seems to have been reached, and at Wells (1258?),[31] Winchester III (1262–65)[32] and Exeter II (1287)[33] the interval was three years. Despite the variations, related perhaps to the size of a diocese and the frequency of episcopal visitations,[34] the legislators were very much in earnest. Several statutes imposed penalties on parents who persisted in negligence,[35] and in his 1281 Provincial Constitutions John Peckham, Archbishop of Canterbury, famously declared:

> Many rashly neglect the further sacrament of confirmation for want perhaps of watchful advisers; so that there are many, innumerable many, who have not yet received the grace of confirmation and are grown old in evil days. To cure this damnable neglect, we ordain that none be admitted to the sacrament of the Lord's Body and Blood that is not confirmed, except at the point of death, unless he has been reasonably impeded from the sacrament of confirmation.[36]

---

[24] Canon xxxvii (PC ii.32).
[25] Canon xxxi (PC ii.71).
[26] Cf. PC ii.32 n.1.
[27] Canon xxxi note e (PC ii.71).
[28] Canon ix (PC ii.369).
[29] Canon xii (PC ii.298).
[30] Canon xi (PC ii.453).
[31] Canon iii (PC ii.591).
[32] Canon iv (PC ii.703).
[33] Canon iii (PC ii.989).
[34] Cf. Fisher BMW, p. 123.
[35] Cf. Canterbury I, Salisbury I, Salisbury II, Worcester III, Wells, etc.
[36] Council of Lambeth, canon iv (PC ii.897).

The Later Middle Ages

As long as infants had been expected to communicate, there was obvious justification for allowing communion before confirmation where bishops were unavailable. But with communion delayed till the age of discretion this justification had lapsed, and Peckham's ruling sought to restore confirmation to its proper place and to re-establish the traditional order of the sacraments. It was not a scandalous innovation as is sometimes suggested,[37] nor did it make confirmation an 'admission to communion' ceremony; indeed the earlier it was administered and the nearer to baptism, the more it was distanced from reception of communion. Where a bishop administered baptism, confirmation might follow immediately but communion would still be delayed for many years.

Peckham's ruling was included in the *Oculus Sacerdotis* of William of Pagula (d c.1332),[38] the *Pupilla Oculi* of John de Burgo (d.1386),[39] the 1430 *Provinciale* of the canonist William Lyndwood[40] and the Sarum and York manuals.[41] Lyndwood's glosses show how gently it was interpreted. On 'neglect' he commented, 'This refers to adults ... for negligence cannot rightly be attributed to those who lack discretion, as do children and infants'. Against 'none' he again said, 'This refers to adults', and on 'impeded' he wrote,

> Because he lacked the opportunity of a bishop to confirm him: or because he was ill and could not get to the place where the bishop was: and thus it is evident that the sacrament of the eucharist can be

---

[37] Cf. e.g. U. T. Holmes, *The Celebration of Maturity in Christ* (Seabury Press, New York, 1975), p. 43f..

[38] In Guildhall Library London (MS 249) pars dextra and pars sinistra, pp. 145, 260 f.; cited A. J. Collins, *Manuale ad usum percelebris ecclesie Sarisburiensis*, (Henry Bradshaw Society, London, 1960), p. 43, n. 61 (Manuale Sarum).

[39] Ed. Paris 1518f, III cap iiB; cited *ibid.*, p. 43, n. 61.

[40] I.6.5, Oxford 1679, p. 40.

[41] *Manuale Sarum, ed. cit.*, p. 43; *York Manual*, ed. W. G. Henderson, (Surtees Society, Durham, 1875), p. 22.

given to a person baptized but not confirmed when it is not his fault that he was not confirmed, and he would have been confirmed if he had not been reasonably impeded.

Lyndwood clearly considered that communion should be refused to the unconfirmed only if they had been guilty of neglect.

St Edmund of Canterbury (c.1180–1240) stated that 'within five years at the latest after an infant has been born, he must be confirmed by the hand of the bishop, and he ought to be well instructed before he be confirmed'.[42] W. Lockton took this to mean that St Edmund invariably demanded instruction before confirmation,[43] but more probably he de-manded it only when confirmation had been delayed for the full 5 years. Nor is it true, as is often claimed, that the Sarum and York manuals suggested 7 as the right age.[44] These manuals still ordered that '[i]f the bishop is present, the infant must be confirmed immediately'.[45] If, as was more usual, the bishop was absent, they laid down in the baptismal charge and the rubrical instructions that confirmation was still to be received 'in all goodly haste' and 'as soon as the bishop shall come within seven miles'.[46] John Myrc in Shropshire (fl 1400) allowed five years as the maximum interval between baptism and confirmation,[47] but Lyndwood

---

[42] *Speculum Ecclesiae* xiv, ed. H. P. Forshaw, (Oxford University Press for the British Academy, London, 1973), p. 65f..

[43] 'The Age for Confirmation' in *Church Quarterly Review* C (1925), pp. 40f..

[44] Cf. E. Daniel, *The Prayer Book* (Gardner, Darton & Co., London, 1905), p. 484; A. J. MacLean, 'The Theory and Practice of Confirmation in the Church up to the Reformation', in *Confirmation or the Laying on of Hands*, ed. Charles J. Ridgway (SPCK, London, 1926f), i.52; C. E. Pocknee, *The Rites of Christian Initiation: Their Revision and Reform* (A. R. Mowbray, London, 1962), p. 33; Fisher BMW, p. 135. The various charges and instructions in the manuals refer to a number of points commonly mentioned in synodical legislation, and their references to the age of 7 and to the learning of the Our Father, Hail Mary and Creed have nothing to do with confirmation.

[45] *Manuale Sarum*, ed. cit., p. 37; *York*, ed. cit., p. 17.

[46] *Sarum*, ed. cit., pp. 32, 37; cf. *York*, ed. cit., p. 21.

[47] *Instructions for Parish Priests*, ed. E. Peacock, Early English Text Society, original series xxxi, rev. edn, F. J. Furnivall, (Kegan Paul, London, 1902), p. 6.

still took 'as quickly as possible' to mean 'within six months',[48] and as late as 1486 Arthur, eldest son of Henry VII, was confirmed on the day of his baptism.[49]

On the continent the situation was even more confusing. Guerric of St Quentin noted the suggestion that the best age was around 7,[50] and William Durandus of Mende (c.1230–96), commenting on a canon (based on an alleged decree of the pseudo-Council of Orleans of 511) which required those of perfect age to confess before confirmation, defined perfect age as 12–15 but recognized that confirmation was often given earlier.[51] In the first imposition of a minimum age the Council of Cologne in 1280 specified '7 or over',[52] as did the Council of Cambrai c.1300–10.[53] The Council of Liege, however, referring in 1287 to '7 or below',[54] implied that 7 was the maximum age, and Walter of Brugghe (1225–1307), who believed that children should not be confirmed till 'they have the use of reason and can know the articles of the faith', also attested the persistence of infant confirmation.[55] The Constitutions of Lucca in 1351, complaining like Peckham of neglect by all ages, also spoke of infant confirmation,[56] while in 1455 a synod at Avignon, recognizing that many people doubted whether confirmation could

---

[48] *Provinciale* i.6.2, ed. cit., p. 34.

[49] J. Stowe, 'Historical Memoranda' in *Three Fifteenth Century Chronicles*, ed. J. Gairdner, (Camden Society, London, 1880), p. 104.

[50] *Quaestiones de Sacramentis*, in Lynch, *op. cit.*, p. 113.

[51] *Rationale Divinorum Officiorum*, vi.8, Corpus Christianorum, Continuatio Mediaevalis, (Brepols, Turnhout, 1966ff.), 140A.433. The canon, was incorporated in Gratian (c.6, C.30, q.1, ed. A. Friedberg, (Tauchnitz, Leipzig, 1879), p. 1414, and read, 'Those fasting should come to confirmation at a perfect age. They should be admonished to make a confession first, that being upright they may be worthy to receive the gift of the Holy Spirit.'

[52] Canon v, Mansi xxiv.349.

[53] Canon *de confirmatione* in J. Hartzheim, *Concilia Germaniae*, (Augustæ Agrippinensium, Cologne, 1759–63), iv.68.

[54] Canon iii.1, Mansi xxiv.889.

[55] *Commentarius in IV Librum Sententiarum* in Lynch, *op. cit.*, p. 169.

[56] Canon xiv, Mansi xxvi.260.

be given to infants, decreed that it could be so administered at the discretion of the bishop.[57] The two practices seem to have coexisted until the Reformation, but with confirmation at 7-plus becoming increasingly common.

2 Instruction, Confession and Age

To enable the discernment and devotion now deemed necessary for admission to communion, instruction was required, and the ending of infant communion coincided with a fresh emphasis on such instruction. Parents[58] and godparents[59] had obvious responsibilities here, but increasingly the teaching role of the clergy was emphasized.[60] The main vehicle of priestly instruction was the sacrament of penance. Annual confession, long customary[61] and now obligatory was 'far more than a mere question of confession and absolution' and was used as 'a thorough-going spiritual examination in faith and morals'.[62] But the formal linking of it with Easter communion strengthened the idea that confession was a necessary

---

[57] Canon xv, Mansi xxiv.187.
[58] St Thomas, *Summa Theologiae* iii.67.7f, ed. Gilby 57.72–79.
[59] Cf. John Myrc, *Instructions for Parish Priests*, ed. Peacock, p. 5; *Sarum, ed. cit.*, pp. 32, 37.
[60] Cf. for England F. A. Gasquet, *Parish Life in Medieval England*, (Methuen & Co, London, ³1909), pp. 213–22, and 'Articles of the Faith', 'Commandments', 'Confession', 'Creed', 'Education', etc in the index to PC.
[61] Cf. J. A. Jungmann, *Handing on the Faith*, (ET, Burns & Oates, London, 1959), p. 14, as against H. C. Lea, *A History of Auricular Confession and Indulgences in the Latin Church*, (Swan Sonnenschein & Co, London, 1896), i.230, and M. Gibbs and J. Lang, *Bishops and Reform 1215–1272, with special reference to the Lateran Council of 1215* (Oxford University Press, London, 1934), p. 97.
[62] J. R. H. Moorman, *Church Life in England in the Thirteenth Century* (Cambridge University Press, Cambridge, 1945), p. 87; cf. also W. A. Pantin, *The English Church in the Fourteenth Century*, (Cambridge University Press, Cambridge, 1955), p. 192; also Winchester I, 1224, canon li (PC ii.134) and Worcester II, 1229, canon viii (PC ii.172); Lincoln, c.1239, canon viii (PC ii.269); Norwich, 1240-3, canon vii (PC ii.346); Winchester II, 1247?, canon x (PC ii.405); Ely 1239-56, canon xiv (PC ii.518); London II, 1245-59, canon lxvii (PC ii.648); Winchester III, 1262-5, canon lix (PC ii.713).

preparation for every communion, and in 1281 Peckham urged priests 'not to minister Christ's body to anyone unless they are sure either by witness or faithful tokens that he is confessed'.[63]

The Lateran Council had stated that confession and communion both became obligatory when children reached *annos discretionis*, one of several terms used for the age at which children attained personal responsibility.[64] It had not defined this age but, according to Jungmann, theologians generally understood it as 'the age at which the child was able to decide between good and bad in moral and intellectual matters to the extent of being *doli capax*, capable of deceit', and they mostly held that this capacity was already present with the seventh year.[65] On this view the obligations began at 7, which was the age suggested at Sisteron c.1244–50.[66]

Some local councils were content, like the Lateran, to speak simply of 'years of discretion',[67] but others defined the age more precisely and none followed Sisteron. Narbonne in 1227,[68] Liege in 1287,[69] Constance in 1300,[70] Cambrai c.1300–10,[71] Lucca in 1308[72] and Avignon in 1341[73] all specified 14 with regard to confession, as in England did Lyndwood,[74] while Tarragona in 1329, dealing with both confession and communion, specified 14 for a boy and 12 for a girl.[75] But the disagreement was more

---

[63] Council of Lambeth, canon ii (PC ii.895).
[64] Others included *aetas congrua, intelligibilis, legitima, perfecta* as well as *usus liberi arbitris*.
[65] *Op. cit* , p. 293, referring to F. Gillmann, 'Die *anni discretionis* im Kanon *Omnis utriusque sexus*', *Archiv für katholisches Kirchenrecht* CVIII (1928). pp. 556–617.
[66] Cf. p. 51f. *supra*.
[67] Cf. Fisher BMW, p. 105.
[68] Canon vii, Mansi xxiii.23.
[69] Canon iv.23. Mansi xxiv.893.
[70] Canon vii, Mansi xxv.31.
[71] Canon *de Poenitentia*, in Hartzheim, *op. cit.*, iv.68.
[72] Canon lvii, Mansi xxv.189.
[73] Canon ii, E. Martene and G. Durand, *Thesaurus Novus Anecdotum* (Paris, 1717), iv.566.
[74] *Provinciale* i.6.2, *ed. cit.*, p. 34.
[75] Canon lxvii, Mansi xxv.870.

apparent than real, for in canon law infancy ended at 7, childhood lasted from 7 to 14, and adulthood followed.[76] All agreed that the obligation was to be assumed at some point in childhood, 7 being the minimum age and 14 the maximum.

For the most part an intermediate age was recommended. St Thomas suggested that communion could be given when children were beginning to show discretion and devotion 'even before they are of perfect age, when they are about 10 or 11',[77] though Durandus, as we have noted, defined 'perfect age', the age at which confirmation should be preceded by confession, as 12–15.[78] The 1280 Council of Cologne suggested that confession should start at 10,[79] and Liege in 1287, while imposing the obligation at 14, suggested communion at 10 and confession at 12.[80] Bayeux in 1300 implied that communion might begin at 7,[81] Cambrai c.1300–10, which again imposed an obligation at 14, suggested communion at 10,[82] but Peter Paludanus (d.1342) argued that the age of discretion was when a child was *doli capax* at around 7 and suggested that both confession and communion should begin then, rather than at puberty which was 14 in a man and 12 in a woman.[83] Later, however, Antoninus (1389–1459) rejected this distinction on the ground that the laws envisaged normal development, and rarely did a child of 7 have the use of reason. A child became capable of sin nearer the future puberty than the past infancy, and puberty occurred at 10 and a half or soon afterwards in a boy and a year or so later in a girl.[84] Angelo de Clavasio (1411–95) favoured a similar age, at least for communion, i.e. in the

---

[76] Cf. W. Lyndwood, *Provinciale* i.6.2, ed. cit., p. 34, and Jungmann, *op. cit*, p. 293f..
[77] *Scriptum super Sententiis* IV dist ix.5.4, ed. Moos iv.394–7.
[78] *Rationale Divinorum Officiorum* vi.8, ed. cit., 140A.433.
[79] Canon v, Mansi xxiv.349.
[80] Canons iii.2 and v.44, Mansi xxiv.889, 899.
[81] Canon xvi, Mansi xxv.63.
[82] Canon *de Eucharistiae*, in Hartzheim, *op. cit.*, iv.73.
[83] *Quartus Sententiarum Liber*, dist xii q.1 a.3 (Paris, 1514), f.49.
[84] *Summa Theologica* iii.9.9 (Venice, 1503), f.269.

tenth or at least the twelfth year, 'when children have the use of reason, when they can conceive some devotion to this sacrament, and discern the body of Christ, and distinguish it from other food'.[85] Savonarola, the Italian reformer (1452–98), quoted St Thomas to the effect that the years of discretion 'begin at the tenth or eleventh year',[86] and the Council of Bamberg in 1496 virtually paraphrased St Thomas, though putting the age back slightly: the Lord's body could be administered to those 'who are beginning to have discretion, even before perfect age — at 11, 12 or 13 — and at other times when signs of devotion, discretion, fervour or longing appear'.[87]

It seems, therefore, that while 14 was the age at which confession and communion normally became obligatory, in many cases both were recommended earlier, sometimes as early as 7. Liege implies that children may occasionally have communicated before confessing, perhaps because the folk-memory of infant communion led parents to bring their children to communion at the first signs of discretion, while postponing confession until discretion was more apparent. But if this did occur, as was quite possible in a period of transition, it was probably rare and short-lived. Jungmann suggests that more generally, and later almost universally, the opposite applied and that 'an earlier age limit was set for first Confession, and a later one for first Holy Communion' on the ground that children became *doli capax* and in need of penance before they attained the deeper devotion and discernment necessary for communion.[88]

3 Summary

Confirmation for strengthening, growth, increase of grace, and the

---

[85] *Summa Angelica de casibus conscientiae, de Eucharistia* iii.12 (Nuremberg, 1488), f.85.
[86] *Confessionale pro instructione confessorum* (Venice, 1543), p.21.
[87] Xxiii. *de Celebratione Missarum et Sacramento Eucharistiae* in Hartzheim, *op. cit.*, v.615.
[88] *Op. cit.*, pp. 294f..

fullness of the Spirit was administered as soon after baptism as possible in England, though later perhaps on the continent. Then, with the dawning of reason and discretion, there followed instruction by priests, parents and sponsors, leading to personal repentance and sacramental confession; further instruction, if necessary, leading to deeper faith, discernment and devotion; and finally, sometime between 7 and 14 and usually perhaps around 12, admission to communion. But the medievals had neither word nor phrase to express the idea of a sequence of initiatory rites extending from baptism to first communion, and only baptism was now strictly initiatory. Confirmation still remained in theory the 'completion' of baptism, but, as it was widely delayed, it lost its initiatory setting, while the rationale of strengthening and growth tended to distance it further and to associate it with a second stage of Christian life. Alexander of Hales (c.1186–1245) and others, seeking to justify its restriction to bishops, declared, 'As catechumens are initiated (*initiantur*, i.e. baptized) by simple priests, they are confirmed (*confirmantur*) by bishops'.[89] When infant communion was abandoned, admission to communion also ceased to be initiatory, and St Thomas explicitly contrasted baptism, the beginning (*principium*) of the spiritual life, with communion as its completion (*consummatio*).[90] Admission to communion was as much a matter of ecclesiastical discipline as of Christian initiation.

---

[89] *Glossa in Quattuor Libros Sententiarum* IV dist vii.6, ed. Collegium Bonaventurae.Quaracchi 1951-7, iv.131. Cf. also Hugh of St Cher, *Commentarius in IV Librum Sentiarum*, Roland of Cremona, *Summa*, and John Moussy, *Commentarius in IV Librum Sententiarum* in Lynch, *op. cit.*, pp. 17, 90, 100.

[90] *Summa Theologiae* iii.73.3, ed. Gilby 58.10-13; cf. also his contrasts between *inchoandam* and *consummandam*, *regeneratur* and *perficitur*, *fundamentum spiritualis vitae* and *vinculum perfectionis*.

B

The Continental Reformation

4 The Reformers

Luther and many later reformers wished to replace the mass by a Lord's Supper which would still be central to the life of the church and at which all eligible would communicate. But they totally misunderstood the hesitations of laypeople, who had rarely communicated more than annually and were not to be dragooned into more frequent communion. Bucer was scornful about such people — 'How can a man communicate other than unworthily … if he will do so only once a year and not then unless compelled by law?' It was his 'hearty desire' that there should be constant teaching about the insult offered to Christ by those who attended but refused to communicate.[1] Calvin also believed that communion should be received as often as it was offered. None were to be compelled but all were to be urged and aroused, and the inertia of the indolent was to be rebuked; he quoted Chrysostom's strictures against those who were present but did not communicate.[2]

As early as 1536 Calvin claimed that from the time of Acts 2 'it became the unvarying rule that no meeting of the church should take place without the Word, prayers, partaking of the Supper, and almsgiving'. The later requirement of communicating only once a year was 'a veritable invention of the devil', and the supper was best observed 'very often and

---

[1] *Censura*, in E. C. Whitaker, *Martin Bucer and the Book of Common Prayer* (Mayhew-McCrimmon for the Alcuin Club, Great Wakering, 1974), pp. 24–30.
[2] *Institutes* (1559) IV.17.44–46; ET J. T. McNeill and F. L. Battles, 1971, ii.1422–5.

at least once a week'.[3] In the following year he referred to 'every Sunday at least as a rule' and explained again from Acts that the supper 'was not instituted by Jesus for making a commemoration two or three times a year, but for a frequent exercise of our faith and charity, of which the congregation of Christians should make use as often as they be assembled'. But, because until recently 'the abomination of the mass' had replaced 'the communion of all the faithful', and 'because the frailty of the people is still so great, there is danger that this sacred and so excellent mystery be misunderstood if it be celebrated so often', he therefore proposed a monthly communion,[4] but this was rejected by the Genevan Council of Ministers 'in favour of a continuation of the customary quarterly observance'.[5] In 1540 he wrote that it should be a well-established custom in all churches 'of celebrating the Supper as frequently as the capacity of the people will allow',[6] and in a 1555 letter to the magistrates of Berne he argued that 'it is a defect in us that we do not follow the example of the Apostles'.[7] Calvin maintained his position consistently, and in 1559 he was still arguing that '[t]he Lord's Table should have been spread at least once a week'.[8] But his approach was essentially pastoral and, having failed to achieve more than quarterly communion, he explained on another occasion, 'I thought it better to indulge a little the people's infirmity, than to contend over-much about it. Nevertheless, I took care to have it entered upon record, that this was an evil custom; to the end that posterity might, with more ease and liberty, correct it.'[9]

John Knox's 1556 *Order of Geneva*, doubtless influenced by Calvin,

---

[3] *Institutes* (1536) IV.40, 53; ET F. L. Battles, (Eerdmans, Grand Rapids, 1986), pp. 112f..

[4] 'Articles concerning the Organization of the Church and of Worship at Geneva 1537' in J. K. S. Reid, *Calvin: Theological Treatises* (SCM, London, 1954), p. 49.

[5] *Ibid.*, p. 47.

[6] 'Short treatise on the Holy Supper' in *ibid.*, p. 153.

[7] Cited by T. David Gordon, 'Why Weekly Communion? in *Ordained Servant* 17 (May 2008), pp. 107–13.

[8] IV.17.43–46; ET McNeill and Battles, 1971, ii.1421–5.

[9] *Resp de quibusd Eccles Ritib*, cited J. Bingham, 'The French Church's Apology for the Church of England' in *Works*, 1845, p.153.

advocated monthly communion, but the *First Book of Discipline* adopted by the General Assembly of the Church of Scotland in 1562 advised quarterly observance in the towns, and twice a year in rural parishes.[10]

Thus, despite the reformers' original intentions, daily, weekly and even monthly celebrations were quickly abandoned. Lay reception remained rare, but it was still deemed a very holy rite. Admission always required instruction, and many catechisms were issued to assist in this.[11] It also required self-examination, and it usually required ministerial examination as well, sometimes with confirmation and/or confession.

It was a group of fifteenth-century Bohemians who, building on the continental delaying of confirmation, first came to understand it as a rite in which children who had been instructed and come to understanding were examined in their faith and then received into the congregation by the laying on of hands with prayer. A confession of 1468 explained that when he is grown up and has come to understanding, so that he can answer for himself, the sureties should then bring him to the pastor, and give testimony concerning him how he has been preserved in the strength of baptism, and has received instruction. Also he should be questioned whether he will so persevere in the faith of the Lord Christ and in the Christian doctrine preached by the apostles. And when it is known that he is of age reckoned according to the testimony of his sureties and his own confession by word of mouth, he shall receive him into the congregation and by laying on of hands confirm him, and pray that God will give him strength from on high with perseverance. And in the old church, he was given a blow on the cheek as a sign that he must suffer for Christ, and this was called Strengthening, whether of old or young. But today in the Roman church they call it Confirmation.[12]

This rite is not explicitly linked with admission to communion but

---

[10] Cf. D. G. Hart and John R. Muether, 'The Lord's Supper: How Often? in *Ordained Servant* 6.4 (October 1997), pp. 97f..

[11] Luther issued catechisms in 1520 and 1529, and Calvin issued catechisms in 1537 and 1541.

[12] In G. Rietschel, *Lehrbuch der Liturgik* (Reuther & Reichard, Berlin, 1909), ii.147, ET W. Lock-

it is implied, then or thereafter, by the statement that the minister 'shall receive him into the congregation'. Again, there is no reference to the Spirit, but a 1504 confession referred to 'an increase of the gifts of the Holy Spirit for steadfastness and the warfare of the faith', and also claimed apostolic precedent for the rite:

> Our faith being taken from the sacred scriptures, we profess that the practice was observed in the times of the apostles. Whoever did not receive the promised gifts of the Holy Spirit in the years of youth received them for the confirmation of faith by prayer and the laying on of hands in this manner. So also we feel with regard to infants. Whoever being baptized has come to the true faith and purposes to portray it in action ... ought to be brought to the bishop, or priest, and be confirmed.[13]

Again, after prayer and the laying on of hands, the newly-confirmed was to 'be received into the fellowship of the church'. The reference to the instances in Acts where the Spirit was given through the laying on of hands some time after baptism was not unreasonable, but there was no justification whatever for linking these with the age of the recipients. Nonetheless this new understanding of confirmation was soon to be widely shared.

Luther initially accepted confirmation as a sacrament,[14] but he soon repudiated this and, while he thought it would be good if there was

---

ton, *art. cit.*, pp. 42f.. The reference to the 'blow on the cheek' in the 'old church' was an odd one in that it appears to have been introduced only at the end of the thirteenth century and was firstattested by Durandus, *op. cit.* VI.84.6–8 (*ed. cit.*, 140A.433). It replaced the kiss of peace at the end of the rite and was apparently taken over from the contemporary knighting ceremony. Durandus explained that its purpose was to help the recipient to remember more clearly his reception of the rite; to strengthen him in his confession of the faith, to remind him of the apostolic imposition of hands and to put to flight the evil spirit.

[13] *Confessio Fidei Fratrum Waldensium*, ET *ibid.*, p. 43.
[14] *In Ep ad Hebreos Comm* 6.f (WA 57.iii.180).

still 'such a laying on of hands as there was in apostolic times, whether we choose to call it confirmation or healing', he argued that it lacked the word of promise required for a sacrament, so it was sufficient to regard it 'as a certain churchly rite or sacramental ceremony, similar to other ceremonies such as the blessing of water'.[15] In 1523 he followed the Bohemians when he stated, 'We do not find fault if every pastor examines the faith of the children to see whether it is good and sincere, lays his hands on them, and confirms them',[16] but many Lutheran church orders were content simply with the examination and profession of faith. In 1535 the Liegnitz Order laid down that children mature in age and grace should confess their faith before the congregation and that 'this is to take the place of confirmation', but it also required further instruction and a further account of their faith before their admission to communion.[17] But this last provision was unusual, and more typical was the 1543 Pfalz-Neuburg Order:

> About a week before Easter, Pentecost and Christmas notice should be given of persons who wish to partake of the Lord's Supper for the first time on the coming feast day. They should be presented on the eve of the holiday and publicly examined at vespers. If they are sufficiently prepared, a common prayer should be offered in their behalf that they grow in faith and doctrine and continue therein to the end. Then the Lord's Prayer should be prayed, after which they may go to the Lord's Supper.[18]

---

[15] *De Captivitate Babylonica Ecclesiae Praeludium* (WA6.549f; LW36.91f); cf. also *Kirchenpostille: Epistel in der Früh* — Christmas (WA10.I.117), cited Fisher RP, p. 172, and, more critically *The Persons related by Consanguinity and Affinity* (LW 45.8f) and *The Estate of Marriage* (LW 45.24f).

[16] *Predigt am Sonntag Lätare Nachmittags* (WA11.66), cited by Repp, *Confirmation in the Lutheran Church*, (Concordia Publishing House, St Louis, 1964), p. 17.

[17] Cf. Repp, *op. cit.*, p. 45.

[18] A. L. Richter, *Die evangelischen Kirchenordnungen des 16 Jahrhunderts* (Weimar, 1846), ii.27, cited *ibid.*, p. 25.

Initially again, Luther accepted penance as a sacrament,[19] but he soon repudiated this too,[20] though he continued to believe it useful and even to recommend it.[21] Despite the church orders, he made little distinction between first communion and subsequent communions, and his real concern was for the worthiness and spiritual understanding of all communicants; instruction was needed to foster these, examination to test them, and sometimes confession to express them. Thus for him catechesis, like confession, 'was not necessarily limited to those contemplating first Communion. Because the average communicant was so poorly instructed, he was to become in effect a catechumen each time he went to Communion'.[22]

Luther was horrified when his fellow-reformer Karlstadt offered the sacrament indiscriminately in 1521,[23] and in 1522 he wrote, 'Even though I do not insist upon it, yet I do advise that you make confession gladly before you go to the sacrament.'[24] In his 1523 *Formula Missae et Communionis* he laid down that, 'lest the worthy and the unworthy alike rush to the Lord's Supper, as we have hitherto seen done in the Roman church', all intending communicants should make personal request to the priest 'so that he may be able to know both their names and manner of life'. None were to be admitted unless they could give a reason for their faith, answer questions about the Lord's Supper and explain their spiritual motivation. It was enough, however, that applicants 'be

---

[19] *The Holy and Blessed Sacrament of Baptism* xv (LW 35.38); cf. also *The Sacrament of Penance* (LW 35.9–22).

[20] *De Captivitate Babylonica Ecclesiae Praeludium*; in WA 6.501 (LW 36.18) penance is one of three sacraments he recognizes, but in WA 6.572 (LW 36.124) he states that '[t]here are, strictly speaking, but two sacraments' and that penance is 'nothing but a way and a return to baptism'. Cf. also WA 6.543–9 (LW 36.81–91).

[21] *De Captivitate Baylonica Ecclesiae Praeludium* (WA 6.546; LW 36.86); cf. also *Eight Sermons at Wittenberg* viii (LW 51.98), *The Sacrament — Against the Fanatics* (LW 26.259), *Confession concerning Christ's Supper* (LW 37.368), *Receiving both Kinds in the Sacrament* (LW 36.258).

[22] Repp, *op. cit.*, p. 22.

[23] *Eight Sermons at Wittenberg* vi (LW 51.92–4).

[24] *Receiving both Kinds in the Sacrament* (LW 36.258).

examined or explored once a year', and it was possible that 'a man may be so understanding that he needs to be questioned only once in his lifetime or not at all. As for private confession before communion, this was 'not necessary or to be demanded, but useful and not to be condemned'.[25] In 1528 he repeated that none should be admitted 'unless he has previously been to the pastor who shall inquire if he rightly understands the sacrament, or is in need of further counsel', and '[i]n examination before the sacrament the people are to be exhorted to make confession, so that they may be instructed where cases of doubt arise in conscience, and may be comforted, when true contrition is in their hearts, as they hear the words of absolution'.[26] The 1530 Augsburg Confession declared that it was not customary to administer the body of Christ 'except to those who have previously been examined and absolved'.[27]

Zwingli claimed that confirmation had arisen only to enable those baptized as infants to profess the faith for themselves, and that for this instruction and examination had been necessary. If these were now omitted, children were worse off than the adult catechumens for whom instruction had been a condition of baptism,[28] but he made no attempt to revive what he deemed this primitive confirmation. In general he emphasized self-examination:

> We ought to examine ourselves before we partake, that is, we ought to search our hearts and ask ourselves whether we have confessed and received Christ as the Son of God our Redeemer and Saviour, so that we trust only in him as the infallible author and giver of

---

[25] *Formula Missae et Communionis* (WA 12.215f; LW 53.32f); cf. also *Instructions for the Visitors of Parish Pastors in Electoral Saxony* (LW 40.292, 296).

[26] *Instructions for the Visitors of Parish Pastors in Electoral Saxony* (LW 40.292, 296).

[27] Art. xxv (Latina invariata, CR 26.302).

[28] *Auslegung des 18. Artikels* (CR 89.122f); cf. also *De Vera et Falsa Religione Commentarius* xx (CR 90.823). Zwingli's historical reconstruction, for which he offered no evidence, differed only in detail from that of the Bohemians.

salvation; and whether we rejoice in the fact that we are members of that Church of which Christ is the head.[29]

There was nothing here about ministerial examination and in 1532, when communion was made compulsory in Zurich, only public sinners under judgment from the magistrates were excluded.[30] Zwingli's disciple, Vadianus, took a similar position in 1536, 'The examination is rightly deemed part of the commemoration, for there can be no commemoration without proper examination',[31] but again this was Pauline self-examination rather than ministerial examination.

Bucer's view of confirmation was much more positive. In 1530 he wrote that, as against the twofold Jewish initiation of circumcision and presentation, the Church had appointed one baptism 'unless you care to add a laying on of hands and solemn blessing such as Christ gave to the children'.[32] In 1531 he suggested that the giving of the Spirit through the laying on of hands had been limited to apostolic times,[33] but in 1533 he included laying on of hands among the gospel sacraments[34] and also cited Jerome in support of a Bohemian-type rite 'whereby those who have grown up and have been adequately instructed in the faith make their profession individually in the presence of the bishop and are, as it

---

[29] *Fidei Christianae Expositio*, eds M. Schuler and J. Schultheiss iv.53–5, ET G. W. Bromiley, *Zwingli and Bullinger* (SCM Press, London, 1955), pp. 258–60.

[30] Cf. E. A. Payne, 'Intercommunion from the Seventeenth to the Nineteenth Centuries' in D. Baillie and J. Marsh (eds), *Intercommunion*, (SCM Press, London, 1952), pp. 87f..

[31] *Aphorismorum de Euchuristiae Consideratione* (Basle, 1536), pp. 14f..

[32] 'Responsiones ad Quaetiones a Georgio Morello et Petro Lathomo Valdensium Provincialum Ablegatis', in J. J. Herzog, 'Ein Wichtiges Document, betreffend die Einführung der Reformation bei den Waldensern', *Zeitschrift für die historische Theologie*, XXXVI (1866). pp. 324 and 337; cf. G. H. Williams, *The Radical Reformation* (Westminster Press, Philadelphia, 1962), p. 522.

[33] 'Apologie der Confessio Tetrapolitana', in *Deutsche Schriften iii.270–2*, cited by W. P. Stephens, *The Holy Spirit in the Theology of Martin Bucer* (Cambridge University Press, Cambridge, 1970), p. 193.

[34] *Quid de Baptismata Infantium Sentiendum* (Strasbourg, 1533), f.A7 and F3a.

were, confirmed by the laying of hands.'[35] Again, in 1534, referring to Jesus' blessing of the children as a sacrament, he implied that the Lord regarded it as of the same standing as baptism,[36] and in the same year he suggested that confirmation be revived in accordance with the ancient custom whereby 'bishops laid their hands on the baptized and thereby gave them the Holy Spirit according to the example of the apostle in Samaria'.[37] At a 1538 synod at Ziegenhain he drew up an *Order of Church Discipline*, which provided that when children were sufficiently instructed to go to the Lord's Table, they should be examined on some high festival in the presence of the congregation. When they had answered the questions and publicly surrendered themselves to Christ and his Church, the congregation was to pray for their perseverance and an increase of the Spirit, and the pastor was to lay his hands on them, 'thus confirming them in the name of the Lord', and to admit them to the Lord's Table.[38] A year later he incorporated these provisions in his Cassel Order, where he explained that the examination was to be on a festival, 'so that the children on whom the hand is laid may go on the same day to the holy supper of Christ'. The laying on of hands was preceded by prayer for the assurance of the Spirit and accompanied by the declaratory formula, 'Receive the Holy Spirit, protection and guard against all evil, strength and help to all goodness from the gracious hand of God.'[39]

---

[35] *Ibid.*, f.F3. But the reference to Jerome was based on a misunderstanding. Jerome, *Dialogus contra Luciferianos* ix (PL 23.172), disliked the rite and said nothing about its being administered simply to those who had grown up and been instructed.

[36] *Katechismus*, in J. M. Reu, *Quellen zur Geschichte des kirchlichen Unterrichts in der evangelischen Kirche Deutschlands zwischen 1530 und 1600* (Olms, Hildesheim, 1976), i.i.42, cited by Repp, *op. cit.*, p. 38.

[37] *Bericht zu Münster* f.L2a, cited by W. P. Stephens, *op. cit.*, p. 193. It is presumably this which Repp, *op. cit.*, p. 30, cites as *Ad Monasterienses* from E. C. Achelis, *Praktische Theologie* (Mohr, Tübingen, 1912), p. 195.

[38] ET Repp, *op. cit.*, p. 31f; cf. also Fisher RP, pp. 179f..

[39] ET Repp, *op. cit.*, pp. 37–9; cf. also Fisher RP, pp. 180f.

Bucer gave the first formal liturgical expression to the link between confirmation and admission to communion. At the same time he provided the first 'Reformation' confirmation rite which, though influenced by a misreading of history and differing significantly from the medieval one, could still claim through its laying on of hands and prayer for the Spirit a real continuity with the past. His sequence of public examination, renewal of baptismal vows, prayer for an increase of the Spirit, laying on of hands, and admission to communion was repeated in Hermann of Cologne's 1543 *Consultation*,[40] and in 1548 he summed up,

> Those who have received baptism before the age of discretion are to be instructed in the faith of Christ by means of the catechism ... until they are able to confess it before the congregation of God. After this they are to be confirmed with the prayer of the whole congregation and (following the Lord's example in Mark 10.16) the laying-on-of-hands, and then also with the holy communion.

He also stated then, though not in specific relation to the supper, that the Lord bestowed special comfort to troubled consciences by means of absolution 'provided that this, whether public or private, is requested and received according to his word', and that 'the people are to value highly both private absolution and instruction, and willingly make use of them'.[41]

Unlike Luther, Bucer distinguished between first communion and subsequent communions. But examination was required for both, and in the *Consultation* he ordered 'that the pastors admit no man to the Lord's

---

[40] ET J. Daye, in Fisher RP, pp. 194–203.

[41] *A Brief Summary of Christian Doctrine* xvii, xx, ET in D. F. Wright, *Common Places of Martin Bucer* (Sutton Courtenay Press, Appleford, 1972), pp. 85, 89. On confession, cf. also *De Regno Christi* i.9, in *Martini Buceri Opera Latina* xv, ed. F. Wendel (Presses universitaires de France, Paris ,1955), p. 75; *De Ordinatione Legitima*, in *Scripta Anglicana*, p. 252.

Supper, which hath not first offered himself to them, and that after he hath first made a confession of his sins, being catechized, he receive absolution according to the Lord's word'. Would-be communicants were to resort to the church the evening before the celebration, and after a 'public institution' on which the pastor listed the categories of men who were not to be admitted, there followed a private instruction of all, one by one.[42]

Meanwhile, probably under Bucer's influence, laying on of hands now became more common among Lutherans. The 1540 Brandenburg Order desired that 'confirmation be retained in accordance with the old practice', which it explained in terms of examination followed by the laying on of hands with prayer.[43] Laying on of hands appeared again in the 1542 Calenberg-Göttingen Order, and with (ambiguous) reference to the Spirit,[44] while a 1545 synod at Stettin decreed that those who were shown, on examination, to know the catechism were 'to be confirmed before the altar with the laying on of hands and thereafter admitted to the Sacrament, which custom was begun among the apostles in Acts'.[45] In the same year the Wittenberg Reformation, drawn up by Melanchthon but also signed by Luther, recognized the value — for doctrine, understanding and discipline — of the confirmation at the age of discretion which consisted of public confession of faith and laying on of hands with prayer.[46] In discussions prior to the 1548 Interim of Leipzig Melanchthon suggested that 14 would be an appropriate age — not that younger children who had been instructed might not be brought by their parents to confession and communion 'in accordance with the passage, "Let the children come to me"', but rather that confirmation should take

---

[42] ET J. Daye, f.cxcv–cc.
[43] ET Fisher RP, pp. 33, 37–9.
[44] Cf. Repp, *op. cit.*, p. 41.
[45] Canon xxiii, J. H. Balthasar, *Erste Sammlung Einiger zur Pommerischen Kirchen-Historie gehörigen Schriften* (Greifswald, 1723–5), i.50.
[46] Cf. Repp, *op. cit.*, p. 49.

place at the age of discretion when children better understood their faith and affirmation. Later he suggested 12 – 15 rather than 14 as the age for confirmation but, whatever the age, his willingness to separate it from first communion is puzzling.[47]

Calvin's attitude to confirmation was much less irenic. In the 1536 *Institutes* he ridiculed medieval confirmation, argued that the 'visible and wonderful graces' of Acts 8 had now ceased and described the concept of increase of grace as 'an overt outrage against baptism'. At the same time he lamented the passing of what he believed was the ancient custom of 'a catechizing, in which children or those near adolescence would give an account of their faith before the church'.[48] In the 1543 *Institutes* he affirmed this primitive catechizing of children and explained that it was to give greater dignity to their examination that the laying on of hands had been added as 'a solemn blessing'. Citing Jerome[49] and Leo I,[50] he warmly approved the (allegedly) ancient practice of that 'laying on of hands, which is done simply as a form of blessing, and wish that it were today restored to pure use'.[51] Later from Hebrews 6.1f he distinguished 'two sorts of catechumens' — heathen adults preparing for baptism, and baptized children of believers preparing for the laying on of hands.[52] He repeated his approval of the ancient practice[53] and his wish that it be 'everywhere restored'.[54] But he himself made no attempt to restore it, and

---

[47] *Ibid.*, pp. 47–50. Repp cited three possible explanations for the separation: a concession to the Romans, a concession to those who did not practise confirmation, or a reflection of an existing separation. But none of these explanations is wholly satisfactory.

[48] V.2–10 (CR 29.141–7; ET *ed. cit.*, pp. 125–30) 1559 IV.19,5–13 (CR 30.1068–75, ET *ed. cit.*, ii.1452–61).

[49] Cf. n. 34 *supra*.

[50] *Ep* clix.7, clxvi.2 (PL 54.1138f, 1194). Leo was actually writing about people who wished to join the catholic church but who had been baptized, not necessarily in infancy, in heretical sects, cf. Fisher, RP, pp. 254–60.

[51] xvi.4 (CR 29.1068f); 1559, IV.19.4 (CR 30.1086f, ET ii.1451f).

[52] *Comm in Ep ad Hebraeos* 6.1f (CR 83.69).

[53] *Comm in Acta* 19,5f (CR 76.443).

[54] *Vera Ecclesiae Reformandae Ratio* (CR 35.629).

only occasionally did he mention children explicitly. In 1537 he ordered that 'the Sunday before the celebration, intimation is to be made in order that no child come before it has made profession of its faith as proved by examination in the catechism',[55] and c.1553 he issued a special catechism for questioning children who wished to receive the supper.[56]

For Calvin, the concept of discipline was crucial,[57] and he was insistent on the examination of potential communicants of every age both by themselves[58] and by the minister.[59] He consistently rejected penance as a sacrament,[60] but he did not abolish it until he had replaced it by examination,[61] and he remained sympathetic to it in a non-Roman form. He continued to recognize that it was sometimes a believer's duty to 'use private confession to his own pastor', and it was his ardent wish to see everywhere 'sheep presenting themselves to their shepherd as often as they wish to partake of the Sacred Supper'.[62] He welcomed believers who deemed themselves unworthy: 'This sacred feast is medicine for the sick, solace for sinners' but 'would bring no benefit to the healthy, righteous, and rich — if such could be found'.[63] But this proper sense of

---

[55] *Articles par les Ministres* (CR 38.7-12). Cf. also *La Forme des Prières Ecclesiastiques* (CR 34.195).

[56] *Catechismus Ecclesiae Genevensis: La Maniere d'Interroguer les Enfans qu'on veut recevoir a la Cene de Nostre Seigneur Jesus Christ* (CR 34.147-60).

[57] Cf. R. N. Caswell, 'Calvin's View of Ecclesiastical Discipline' in G. E. Duffield (ed.), *John Calvin* (Sutton Courtenay Press, Appleford, 1966), pp. 210-26.

[58] Cf *Institutio* 1536, iv.36-8 (CR 29,127-9, ET pp. 150-2); 1559, IV.17-40-2 (CR 30.1042-5, ET ii.1418-20); also 1559 IV.16.31 (CR 30.998, ET ii.1153); *Petit Traicte de la Saincte Cene* (CR 33.441-7).

[59] Cf. *Institutes* 1559, IV.17.43 (CR 30.1046, ET ii.1421); also IV.12.5 (CR 30.907, ET ii.1232); *La Forme des Prières Ecclesiastiques* (CR 34.195-8); *Articles par les Ministres* (CR 38.10); *Ep* ccxviii (1540, CR 39.41), *Ep* ccxiv (1540, CR 39.31); *Ep*.1085 (1540; CR 41.76).

[60] *Institutes* 1536 V.11-44 (CR 29,147-77, ET pp. 177-216); 1559, enlarged, III.3.1-4.39, IV. 19.14-17, CR 30.434-90, 1075-8, ET i.592-669, ii.1461-5).

[61] *Ep* ccxviii (1540, CR 39.41); cf. also *Ep* ccxiv, CR 39.31).

[62] *Institutes* 1559 III.4.12-14, based on additions to the 1539 and 1543 editions (ET i.636-9). Cf. also *Secunda Defensio de Sacramentis Fidei*, where he stated 'It is not my purpose to deny that private absolution is useful.' (CR 37.102).

[63] *Institutes* 1536 iv.37f, ed. cit., pp. 111f.

unworthiness was wholly different from the unworthiness of the self-righteous, the casual and the scandalous. In 1537 he emphasized that the sacrament must be protected from profanation and prostitution, that it was necessary 'that they who come to this communion be approved members of Jesus Christ' and that 'for this reason our Saviour set up in his church the correction and discipline of excommunication'.[64] He further insisted that when the minister recited the promises which were left to us in the Supper, 'at the same time, he should excommunicate all who are debarred from it by the Lord's prohibition'.[65]

In 1540, from his exile in Strasbourg, he explained to Farel that it was his practice when the day of the sacrament drew near, to 'give notice from the pulpit that those who are desirous to communicate must first of all let me know'. It would be shameless effrontery 'for any one not even to condescend to avouch his faith in the face of the church with whom he sought communion', the Church would be in a wretched state 'if it could be compelled to receive ... those of whom it is altogether ignorant, or perhaps regards with suspicion', and the minister, 'to whom the dispensation of this grace is committed on condition that he may not cast it before dogs and swine, that he must not pour it out to the worthy and unworthy without distinction' could not perform his onerous duty without 'some fixed and certain method for separating the worthy from the unworthy communicants'.[66] On his return to Geneva he continued to press for the proper examination of all communicants[67] and to stress that the sacrament must be protected from profanation and pollution,[68] and in 1549 he wrote to Somerset in England that 'the duty of bishops

---

[64] *Articles par les Ministres* (CR 38.10).
[65] *Institutio* 1536, iv.53 (CR 29,140, ET p. 167); 1559, IV.17.43, (CF 30.1046, ET ii.1421). Cf. also *La Forme des Prières Ecclesiastiques* (CR 34.198).
[66] *Ep* ccxviii (1540, CR 39.41); cf. also *Ep* ccxiv, CR 39.31).
[67] Cf. *Projet d'Ordonnances Ecclesiastiques* (CR 38.15f) and *La Forme des Prières Ecclesiastiques* (CR 34.195).
[68] *Institutio* 1543 viii.188 (CR 30.660f); 1559, IV.12.5, CR 30.907, ET ii.1232).

and curates is to keep watch over discipline so that the Lord's Supper may not be polluted by people of scandalous lives'.[69] For the rest of his ministry he fought hard not only to establish discipline in Geneva but also to win for the church as against the Senate the final authority in it.[70]

To sum up, none of the reformers apart from Zwingli wanted to abolish the fencing which the medievals had maintained against unqualified communicants. They sought rather to strengthen the materials and where they deemed them inadequate or unscriptural to replace them with something firmer — essentially the examination (public before first communion), which was concerned equally with knowledge and profession and tested both instruction and commitment. The resulting pattern (except for Melanchthon) was baptism, instruction, examination sometimes with private confession of sins but always with public confession of faith, prayer sometimes accompanied by the laying on of hands, and finally admission to communion. But with further examinations normally required before subsequent communions just as further confession had been required in the past, the examination was nearer to the medieval confession than to the once-for-all medieval confirmation, and, Bucer apart, it was confused with confirmation in a way that confession had never been.

In requiring that confirmation, where retained, should be preceded by instruction, the reformers believed that they were returning to scriptural or patristic usage. Historically they were absurdly wrong, but this does not mean that their procedures were pastorally or even theologically wrong. It was no new demand that infants when they grew up should own the faith into which they had been baptized. The medievals had enabled them to do this in the confessional, and their first communion

---

[69] *Ep* 1085 (CR 41.76).
[70] Cf. the documents cccvii–ccxviii, in B. J. Kidd, *Documents Illustrative of the Continental Reformation* (Oxford University Press, Oxford, 1967), pp. 629–51.

(once infant communion had been abolished) and all their subsequent communions were a public attestation of this. But confession was a private owning of a promise formerly made for them publicly, while communion was a ritual owning of a promise formerly made for them verbally. The reformers' examination enabled their owning to be both public and verbal, and the public and verbal profession which had preceded baptism and communion in early adult initiation was now made after baptism but still before communion. It was this public examination and profession of faith before admission to communion which was the distinctive feature of the reformers' demands, and it was the linking of this with the laying on of hands and prayer for the Spirit which was the distinctive achievement of Bucer.

5   The Roman Response

At least one Roman, Erasmus, had some sympathy with the reformers. He still upheld the medieval doctrine of confirmation, but he hoped that infant confirmation which still persisted in some regions would cease as infant communion had already ceased. He thought that confirmation was best given sometime after 7, when children began to incline towards sin, and first communion at about 16, when the devil directed all his cunning against Christ's soldiers.[71] Confirmation was not therefore an 'admission to communion' ceremony and, though it would presumably be preceded by basic instruction, there would be further instruction in the years before communion. In 1522, influenced perhaps by the Bohemians,[72] he proposed that each Lent children who had reached puberty should

---

[71] *Dilucida et Pia Explanatio Symboli* in *Opera Omnia*, ed. J. Leclerc (Leyden 1703–6), v.1175f. Cf. also on confirmation *Paraphrasis in Acta Apostolorum* 8.15f, *ibid.*, vii.699.

[72] For the contact between Erasmus and the Bohemians, cf. J. K. Zeman, *The Anabaptists and the Czech Brethren in Moravia 1526–1628* (Mouton, The Hague, 1969), pp. 137–40, and J. B. Payne, *Erasmus: His Theology of the Sacraments* (John Knox Press, Richmond, VA, 1970), p. 313. But Erasmus did not link his suggested public profession and ratification with confirmation, as they did.

be ordered to attend catechetical sermons on the baptismal profession. They should then be privately examined and, if they showed sufficient understanding, they should be asked whether they ratified what their godparents had promised: 'If they say that they do, then let that profession be renewed in public at a gathering of their equals, and that with solemn ceremonies, fitting, pure, serious, and magnificent' — and these would have greater authority if performed by the bishops rather than by parish priests or hired suffragans. It was common to put on plays in churches, showing the resurrection, the ascension and the descent of the Spirit,

> but how much more glorious a spectacle it would be to hear the voices of so many youths dedicating themselves to Christ, so many initiates pronouncing their vows, renouncing the world, abjuring Satan; to see new Christians bearing the mark of the Lord on their foreheads, to behold the great crowds of candidates coming up from the sacred laver, to hear the voices of the multitude acclaiming the beginners in Christ.

To some this might seem a repetition of baptism, but it would be no more so than daily sprinkling with holy water and would be better regarded as a kind of restoration and representation of it.[73] A more serious problem was that some children, having heard what others had professed for them, might not wish to ratify it. Here there should be no compulsion and no penalty 'other than that of being forbidden to receive the eucharist and the other sacraments' until they came to a right mind. The problems were not insurmountable, and if the practice were adopted, 'we should not have so many who at the age of 50 do not know

---

[73] R. H. Bainton, *Erasmus of Christendom* (Collins, London, 1970), p. 314, regards this distinction between 're-enactment' and 'repetition' as 'purely verbal' and adds that 'it is not too far-fetched to say that he was the only Anabaptist in the sixteenth century, because the Anabaptists insisted that they were simply Baptists, not Anabaptists, since the first baptism in their eyes was no baptism at all'.

what was vowed for them in baptism, and who have not the faintest idea of the meanings of the creed, the Lord's Prayer and the sacraments'.[74]

Calvin partially defended Erasmus,[75] though some catholics quickly accused him of inventing a new sacrament and of denying the church's authority over her children.[76] Many of them, however, shared his dislike of infant confirmation, and the 1536 Council of Cologne, summoned by Hermann in his catholic days, commended what it understood as the recommendations of the [pseudo] 511 Council of Orleans

> namely, that persons should come fasting to confirmation, and of a perfect age, so that they may be admonished to make sacramental confession before they come to it, whereby purified they may be worthy to receive the gift of the Holy Spirit. For since this sacrament is not of absolute necessity, it will be given more profitably, if a little admonition may be added. But before an infant has advanced beyond the seventh year of his age, he will understand, not to say remember, too little or nothing of those things that are done.[77]

In its 1547 *Decree concerning the Sacraments* the Council of Trent without mentioning Erasmus by name condemned his distinctive suggestions:

> That those who have been thus baptized when infants are, when they have grown up, to be questioned whether they will ratify what their sponsors promised in their name when they were baptized; and that, if they answer that they will not, they are to be left to their own will,

---

[74] *Paraphrasis in Evangelium Matthaei, praefatio, ibid.*, v.3v.,

[75] 'What they disapprove dropped on some occasion from Erasmus, perhaps without much consideration. Yet a candid interpreter would only desire some correction in the terms, and conclude that their author was not fully conversant in the government of the church', in *Acts Synodi Trideninae cum Anidoto* (CR 35.501).

[76] Cf. Payne, *op. cit.*, pp. 173f, 314f..

[77] Council of Cologne ix, ET Fisher RP, p. 185. For the text of the canon and the contemporary misunderstanding of it, cf. note 11 *supra*.

and are not meanwhile to be compelled to a Christian life by any other penalty, save that they be excluded from participation in the eucharist and in the other sacraments.[78]

The Council was equally unsympathetic to the protestant reformers and the same decree condemned anyone who asserted

> that the confirmation of the baptized is an idle ceremony, and not rather a true and proper sacrament; or that it was formerly nothing more than a kind of catechism whereby those who were near years of discretion declared an account of their faith in the face of the church.[79]

Its catechism repeated that confirmation, at present 'altogether omitted by many', should be omitted by no one. It was a sacrament by whose grace 'we grow to full maturity' and by whose virtue 'the faithful increase, and acquire perfect spiritual strength'. It was given both to perfect and increase the grace of baptism. As for the age of the recipients,

> After baptism, the sacrament of confirmation may indeed be administered to all; but until children shall have attained the use of reason, its administration is inexpedient. Wherefore, if not to be postponed to the age of twelve, it is most proper to defer this this sacrament at least to that of seven; for confirmation has not been instituted as necessary to salvation, but that by virtue thereof we might be found very well armed and prepared, when called upon to fight for the faith of Christ; and for this kind of conflict assuredly no one will consider children, who still want the use of reason, to be qualified.[80]

---

[78] *Canones de sacramento baptismi* xiv, in H. Denzinger, *Enchiridion Symbolorum Definitionum et Declarationum*, A Schönmetzer (Herder, Barcelona, 32nd. rev., edn, 1963), n. 1626fm, p. 384.
[79] *Canones de sacramento confirmationis* i–ii, in Denzinger, *op. cit.*, nn. 1628–30, p. 384.
[80] Ii.3, ET J. Donovan (Dublin nd [c.1829]), pp. 175–86.

The Council also upheld the sacramental status of penance and reaffirmed the Lateran requirement,[81] while its catechism declared

> No one is bound by the law of confession, before that age at which he can have the use of reason, a time, however, that has not been defined by any fixed number of years: but it seems to be laid down as a general principle that a child is bound to go to confession as soon as he is able to distinguish between good and evil, and his mind is capable of malice.[82]

Since the catechism expected all confirmation candidates to have the use of reason, it clearly required confession to precede confirmation, but it was ambiguous as to whether confirmation was always to precede communion. But though in many places opportunities for receiving confirmation were still strictly limited, the catechism said nothing to suggest that confirmation was to be delayed intentionally till after first communion, and its ideal scheme would seem to be baptism, instruction, confession, confirmation, examination (by father and confessor) and first communion.

---

[81] *Doctrina de Sacramento Paenitentiae*, Denzinger, *op. cit.*, nos. 1670–83, pp. 391–6, and canons i–viii, *ibid.*, 1701–8, pp. 401f..
[82] Ii.5, *ed. cit.*, pp. 247–50.

C

The Church of England

6 The Henrician Reformation

Continental attitudes soon found their way to England, and in 1530 penance and confirmation as traditionally understood[1] were rejected by Tyndale, who claimed from 'probable conjectures and evident tokens' that originally children of 11 or 12 and already well instructed by their priest, 'before they were admitted to receive the sacrament of Christ's body' were examined by a higher officer who then confirmed their baptism and put the sign of the cross on their foreheads.[2] In 1536 the Lower House of Canterbury Convocation found it necessary to complain of 67 *Mala Dogmata* currently being propagated; these included 'that children ought not in any wise to be confirmed of the bishops afore they come to the age of discretion' and 'that auricular confession, absolution and penance, are neither necessary nor profitable'.[3] In general, though, traditional attitudes both to confirmation and to penance remained prevalent. Tyndale lamented the continuing popularity of infant confirmation,[4] but in 1533 Henry had his daughter Elizabeth confirmed — by Cranmer no less — immediately after her baptism when only three

---

[1] *The Obedience of a Christian Man*, in *Doctrinal Treatises* (*Works*, ed. H. Walter, PS, i.273–83).
[2] *Answer to More*, ibid., iii.71f.
[3] Nos. iv and xxvi in T. Fuller, *Church History of Britain*, v. 4, new ed. J. S. Brewer (Oxford University Press, Oxford, 1845), iii.127–36.
[4] *Answer to More, ed. cit.*, iii.72.

days old,[5] while the 1537 *Bishops' Book*, commended people presenting their children 'when they be of so tender age, as commonly they be wont to do',[6] though this was omitted in the 1543 *King's Book*.[7] But even now Cranmer was arguing cautiously that confirmation was not a sacrament, was not instituted by Christ and was not based on apostolic precedent. Chrism was an ordinance of the church not of the scriptures, and he questioned whether it was essential for it to be administered by a bishop. More positively, 'The bishop, in the name of the church, doth invoke the Holy Ghost to give strength and constancy, with other spiritual gifts, unto the person confirmed; so that the efficacy of this sacrament (sic) is of such value as is the prayer of the bishop made in the name of the church.'[8] As for penance, the Ten Articles of 1536 described it as a sacrament 'necessary for man's salvation',[9] and this was repeated in the *Bishops' Book*,[10] the Six Articles of 1539[11] and the *King's Book*.[12]

Public examination was first required by Latimer, whose 1537 Injunctions for Worcester forbade priests to admit any young person 'until that he or she openly in the Church, after mass or Evensong, upon the holiday, do recite in English the *Pater*'.[13] The requirement of the *Pater* was minimal, but the insistence on young people reciting it openly in the church rather than privately in the confessional was very significant. Other

---

[5] C. Wriothesley, *A Chronicle of England during the Reigns of the Tudors*, ed. W. D. Hamilton, (Camden Society, London, 1875), i.22f..

[6] *Formularies of Faith*, ed. C. Lloyd (Oxford University Press, Oxford, 1825), p. 96.

[7] *Ibid*, p. 290.

[8] *Collection of Tenets from the Canon Law*, in *Miscellaneous Writings and Letters*, ed. E. Cox, PS, pp. 74f.; *Some Queries concerning Confirmation*, ibid., p. 80.

[9] *Ibid.*, pp. 6–10.

[10] *Ibid.*, pp. 92–100.

[11] No. lxv in H. Gee and W. J. Hardy, *Documents Illustrative of English Church History* (Macmillan, London, 1896), p. 306.

[12] *Formularies of Faith*, pp. 257–62.

[13] No.10, W. H. Frere and W. M. Kennedy, *Visitation Articles and Injunctions of the Period of the Reformation* (Longmans, Green & Co, London, 1910), ii.17. Frere and Kennedy reprint the full corpus of articles and injunctions up to 1575.

injunctions continued to require private examination in the confessional of all intending communicants,[14] but in 1538 three other bishops made specific reference to young people. Shaxton of Salisbury ordered that young people be taught the *Pater*, Creed and Commandments, and that none of them be admitted to the sacrament until they could 'perfectly say and rehearse' them 'wheresoever they be shriven'.[15] Voysey of Exeter likewise ordered each curate to examine his youth in these same formulae, plus the *Ave* and the seven works of mercy, 'when he admitteth any of them to the Blessed Sacrament of the altar'.[16] But Cranmer, in injunctions for Hereford, followed Latimer in requiring open recitation and forbade priests to admit any young people to the sacrament 'which never received it before' until they had recited the formulae 'openly in the Church, after mass, or Evensong, upon the holy-day'.[17] This was the first injunction specifically to mention first communion, though it was probably implicit in the others. But Cranmer was untypical and until Henry's death the official pattern was the same as in medieval times, and children were admitted to communion after baptism, confirmation, instruction and confession with private examination.

7 The Edwardine Reformation

Prior to the accession of Edward VI in 1547, Cranmer and other would-be English reformers had enjoyed significant doctrinal discussions but they seem to have given little thought as to what a protestant church might be like in practice and to have learned little from developments on the continent. They initially envisaged the continuance of a daily mass but with others communicating alongside the priest. They seem

---

[14] Rowland Lee of Coventry and Lichfield, 1537, nos 8–10, *ibid.*, ii.21f; Royal Injunctions, 1538, no 5, *ibid.*, ii.37; Edward Lee of York, 1538, no 4, *ibid.*, ii.45.
[15] No. 11, *ibid.*, ii.56.
[16] No. 8, *ibid.*, ii.63.
[17] No. 7, *ibid.*, ii.66.

likewise to have envisaged the mass as the principal Sunday service; it was here that notices were to given and the sermon to be preached, and it was the epistles and gospels but not the lessons for Morning and Evening Prayer that were included in the prayer books. But like the continentals they totally misunderstood the unwillingness of the people to communicate more frequently. Contrary to their initial hopes, even a weekly administration was normally replaced by a monthly or quarterly one or even something less frequent than that. As on the continent, reception of communion was almost as rare as it had been previously.

On Edward's accession a new set of Royal Injunctions was issued, and examination in the confessional each Lent was still required before reception of communion.[18] Charity was also required, and there was long precedent for this. An early medieval canon had stated,

> It has been decreed that of persons at variance none venture to draw near to the Altar of the Lord, or to receive the grace of holy communion, until he be reconciled ... But if one of them, though the other despise it, shall have met his adversary for the satisfaction of charity, let him be received into the Church as a peacemaker from the time that he is proved to have made effort for concord.[19]

Similarly, a pre-Reformation communion exhortation, the script of which 'seems to be of a date somewhat later than 1500',[20] read:

> I charge you if there be any man or woman that beareth in his heart any wrath or rancour to any of his fellow-Christians that he be not houselled until the time that he be in perfect love and charity with

---

[18] No.9, Frere and Kennedy, *op. cit.*, ii.119.
[19] Ed. S. Balusius, *Capitularia Regum Francorum*, bk 7 can 242 (Paris 1677), i.1076.
[20] H. A. Wilson, in *The Order of the Communion* (Henry Bradshaw Society, London, 1908), p. xv.

him, for whoso beareth wrath or evil will in heart to any of his fellow-Christians is not worthy his God to receive, and if he do so, he receiveth his damnation where he should receive his salvation.[21]

In the spirit of these, the Injunctions now declared,

> Forasmuch as variance and contention is a thing which most displeaseth God, and is most contrary to the blessed Communion of the Body and Blood of our Saviour Christ, curates shall in no wise admit to the receiving thereof any of their cure or flock, who hath maliciously and openly contended with his neighbour, unless the same do first charitably and openly reconcile himself again, remitting all rancour and malice, whatsoever controversy hath been between them.[22]

Later in 1547 the Sacrament Act laid down a new procedure for occasions, presumably now to be more frequent, when communion was to be offered to laypeople. At least a day before he ministered the sacrament the priest was to exhort those present to prepare themselves. Then on the day appointed there would be a godly exhortation on the importance of receiving worthily so that each man 'shall try and examine his own conscience' before he received, and, that done, the minister 'shall not, without lawful cause, deny the same to any person that will devoutly and humble desire it'.[23] There was no reference here to private confession or ministerial examination being required.

The 1548 *Order of the Communion* again envisaged more frequent lay communion and provided that the parson 'the next Sunday or holyday,

---

[21] Harleian MS 2383 in W. Maskell, *Monumenta Ritualia Ecclesiae Anglicanae* (Oxford, 1882), iii.408.
[22] No. 25 in Frere and Kennedy, *op. cit.*, ii.19.
[23] Gee and Hardy, *op. cit.*, p. 322.

or at the least, one day before he shall minister the Communion, shall give warning to his parishioners, or those which be present, that they prepare themselves thereto'. An exhortation was provided urging them to come with repentance and faith, and having reconciled themselves to any whom they had offended, or been offended by, and having put away all hatred and malice. Any whose consciences were troubled were further invited to make confession to a priest and receive comfort and absolution. Those who were satisfied with a general confession were not to be offended with those who did this; equally those who did so were not to be offended with those who did not. In the rite itself, the people were to be communicated immediately after the priest who was to exhort them to receive worthily, and urge,

> If any man here be an open blasphemer, an adulterer, in malice, or envy or any other notable crime, and be not truly sorry therefore and earnestly minded to leave the same vices, or that doth not trust himself to be reconciled to almighty God, and in charity with all the world, let him yet a while bewail his sins and not come to this holy table.

He was to pause a while to see if any would withdraw, and if anyone did he was to commune with him privately at a convenient time and see 'whether he can with good exhortation, bring him to grace'.

There then followed the invitation, 'Ye that do truly', which stressed the requirements of repentance, charity and faith, and this was followed by a general confession and absolution.

The 1549 Prayer Book also envisaged continued celebration on Sundays and holydays, and in some places daily, but there were always to be 'some' to communicate with the priest and this was ensured on Sundays by a rota system. When there were no communicants, the priest was to conclude the service after the offertory with one or two collects and a blessing. The introductory rubrics to the service laid down that intending communicants should signify their names to the curate 'overnight: or else in the morning, afore the beginning of Matins, or immediately after'. This enabled the curate to know whether there would be some communicants and also to vet the names of those who had signified and

> [i]f any of those be an open and notorious evil liver, so that the congregation by him is offended, or have done any wrong to his neighbours by word or deed: The Curate shall call him, and advertise him, in any wise not to presume to the Lord's Table, until he have openly declared himself to have truly repented, and amended his former naughty life.

He was to use the same procedure 'with those betwixt whom he perceiveth malice, and hatred to reign, not suffering them to be partakers of the Lords table until he know them to be truly reconciled'.[24] If, however, one party was content to forgive while the other remained 'in his forwardness and malice', he was to admit the penitent person but not 'him that is obstinate'.

1548–49 thus made two decisive breaks with the medieval pattern. First, communion could now be received without previous sacramental confession, though confession was still an option. In addition to the reference in the advance notification of administration, a rubric in the visitation of the sick provided that 'here shall the sick person make a special confession, if he feel his conscience troubled with any weighty matter', and a form of absolution was then printed which was to be 'used in all private confessions'. Secondly, people could no longer enjoy their mass unless some of them were prepared to communicate with the priest. But while 1549 repeated the medieval insistence on reception at least once a year, Cranmer like the continentals wanted it to be received more

---

[24] Ridley's 1550 articles enquired whether this procedure was being observed; art. 36, Frere and Kennedy, *op. cit.*, ii.236; cf. also Arthur Bulkeley, art. 22, *ibid.*, ii.264.

frequently, though there was a tension here between frequent reception and worthy reception. He rejected at this stage what he understood to be the primitive requirement that everyone present should receive communion, and he explained to the Devon rebels,

> Although I would exhort every good christian man often to receive the holy communion, yet I do not recite all those things to the intent, that I would in this corrupt world, when men live so ungodly as they do, that the old canons should be restored again, which command every man present to receive the communion with the priest, which canons, if they were now used, I fear that many would receive it unworthily.[25]

In the past the worthiness of communicants had been ensured, at least in theory, by the requirement of private confession. This was now optional, but on Sundays and holydays the curate was instructed, after the sermon or homily, to read the 1548 exhortation on the importance of worthy reception (unless this had already been referred to), and if the people were negligent to come he was give notice of his intention to offer communion 'on … next' in the words of the other 1548 exhortation which emphasized the importance of repentance and invited those whose consciences were troubled to make private confession.

But the advance signifying of intention to communicate was still only a signifying. It did not normally involve the examination favoured on the continent, and in 1551 Daniele Barbaro, the Venetian ambassador, claimed that it was 'ordained in the book, but not observed, having been done for appearance sake'.[26] Hooper of Gloucester, however, was insistent

---

[25] 'Answer to the Fifteen Articles of the Rebels' in *Miscellaneous Writings and Letters*, p. 172.
[26] Report, May 1551, *Calendar of State Papers*, Venetian, no. 703, Vol. V (1534–54), ed. R. Brown, 1873, p. 348.

that the unworthy should be repelled.[27] In his 1551 Visitation Articles, he went beyond 1549 and required that all intending communicants should rehearse the Commandments and Articles of Faith, make the general confession set forth in the prayer book, and say the Lord's Prayer in English. If there were too many to say them individually, they were to repeat them together after the curate.[28] Bucer, in a letter to Hooper, lamented that the ignorant were not instructed in the catechism, and those who had made confession of faith neither by word or deed were still admitted to the supper.[29] Later, in his *Censura*, he described the introductory rubrics as 'of the greatest value to the health of the church', and declared that the Spirit of Christ could not dwell in those who even after full explanation were vexed by the demand that they should indicate to their pastor their wish to communicate.[30] The rota system and the requirement of annual communion should be replaced by an exhortation to pastors to teach their people to communicate whenever there is a celebration. If public teaching proved fruitless, it must be followed by private admonition and entreaty and those who still refused should be excommunicated.[31]

1552 made no change in the requirement of signifying intention,[32]

---

[27] *A Brief and Clear Confession* xi, xlvii–xlix, lviii–lxii, lxx, lxxii–lxv, in *Later Writings*, ed. C. Levinson, PS, pp. 25, 40f, 45–7, 50–2.

[28] No. 9, Frere and Kennedy, *op. cit.*, ii.282; cf. also no 11, *ibid.*, ii.283, where he further ordered that all parishioners should make open confession of the formularies four times a year.

[29] *De Re Vestaria*, in *Scripta Anglicana*, pp. 795f..

[30] *Censura, ed. cit.*, p. 18.

[31] *Ibid.*, pp. 24–30.

[32] In Walter Haddan's 1560 Latin version of the (1559) prayer book, published under the authority of the Queen, the closing words of the first rubric read *immediate post principium matutinarum precum*. But Hadden was a careless translator (cf. Cuming, *op. cit.*, p. 124); such an interruption of Mattins can hardly have been intended, and the natural sense – 'after morning prayer' – is obviously the right one. Text in *Liturgical Services of the Reign of Queen Elizabeth*, ed. W. K. Clay, PS, p. 383. Cf. also F. Procter and W. H. Frere, *A New History of the Book of Common Prayer* (Macmillan & Co, London, 1905), pp. 117–25, and F. Streatfield, *Latin Versions of the Book of Common Prayer* (Mowbray, London, 1964), pp. 2–7.

but it strengthened the demand for worthiness by the addition of the Ten Commandments with expanded *kyries* and, although it abandoned the Sunday rota system, it strengthened the demand for more frequent reception by insisting that 'a good number' should communicate with the priest, as against the 'some' of 1549, that 'in Cathedral and Collegiate churches, where be many Priests and Deacons, they shall all receive the Communion with the minister every Sunday at the least, except they have a reasonable cause to the contrary', and that every parishioner should now communicate 'at least three times in the year: of which, Easter to be one'. Cranmer also introduced a new exhortation, influenced by Peter Martyr,[33] to be read after the prayer for the church militant at 'times when the Curate shall see the people negligent to come to the holy Communion'. This assumes that communion will be administered for it begins, 'We be come together at this time … to feed at the Lord's supper'.[34] It stresses the divine invitation, begs the people to communicate and not to 'stand by as gazers and lookers on at them that do' and bids those who will not communicate to 'depart you hence'. Cranmer clearly hoped that some who had not previously intended to communicate

---

[33] Cf. Cuming, *op. cit.*, p. 99.
[34] The exhortations may be summarized thus (*italicized entries refer to future celebrations*).

1548

1. *Dear Friends, and you especially*	*A warning of intention to administer within a week*
2. Dearly beloved in the Lord, ye coming	To communicants before 'Ye that do truly'
3. If any man here	Immediately after no.2

1549

1. Dearly beloved in the Lord, ye that mind	To communicants after sermon (nos 2 and 3 of 1548)
2. *Dear Friends, and you especially*	*A warning of intention to administer within a week, if negligent (no 1 of 1548)*

1552

1. We be come together	To negligent after prayer for church if necessary (new)
2. Dearly beloved, forasmuch	Sometime also, at his discretion (no 2 of 1549)
3. Dearly beloved in the Lord, ye that mind	To communicants always (no 1 of 1549).

would now do so, although this seems contradictory to the requirement of advance signification.

Some writers were not unsympathetic to private confession in what they deemed the right circumstances,[35] though Hooper in his 1551 Visitation Articles, enquired whether any ministers taught auricular confession or required it of communicants,[36] in his diocese it was apparently not optional but forbidden. 1552 now carried further 1549's minimizing of it. A general confession and absolution, already included in the communion service, was prefixed to morning and evening prayer, and the pre-communion invitation to private confession was now given only to 'any of you which by the means aforesaid [i.e. self-examination, confession to God and reconciliation to neighbours] cannot quiet his own conscience'.[37] But private confession as a preliminary to communion was still not generally replaced by strict ministerial examination. It was only 'having knowledge thereof' that the curate was to summon open and notorious evil livers who signified their intention to communicate, and in any case the gap between the ending of Morning Prayer — the last time for signification — and the beginning of Communion was too brief to allow proper examination. There was emphasis on the importance of self-examination,[38] but no warrant as yet for Genevan snooping or ministerial prying.

Cranmer now issued an English version of a Lutheran catechism by

---

[35] Cf. Ridley, Ep.vi, 1554, in *Works*, ed. H. Christmas, PS, p. 338; Roger Hutchinson, 'The Image of God' vii, xvii, xxx in *Works*, ed. J. Bruce, PS, pp. 44, 86f, 199, and 'First Sermon on the Lord's Supper' in *ibid.*, p.243f; Hugh Latimer, 'Sermons' xxii, xxx, xl in *Sermons*, ed. G E Corrie, PS, p. 423 and *Sermons and Remains*, ed. G. E. Corrie, PS, pp. 12f, 179f..

[36] Nos. 37 and 56, in Frere and Kennedy, *op. cit.*, ii.297f..

[37] The word 'secretly' was deleted from the invitation, as was the 1549 statement that the absolution printed in the Visitation of the Sick was to be used 'in all private confessions'. The absolution itself was still printed, but the priest was only ordered to absolve 'after this sort'.

[38] Cf. J. Bradford, 'Sermon on the Lord's Supper' in *Writings*, ed. A. Townsend, PS, i.108f; R Hutchinson, 'First Sermon of the Lord's Supper' in *Works*, pp. 225f.; J. Hooper, 'Sermons upon Jonas' vi in *Early Writings*, ed. S. Carr, PS, pp. 535f..

Justus Jonas, and his preface explained that there would have been little need for Reformation if the education of young people had not been so neglected or

> if the ancient and laudable ceremony of confirmation had continued in the old state, and been duly used of the ministers in time convenient, where an exact and strait examination was had of all such as were of full age, both of their profession that they made in baptism touching their belief and keeping of God's commandments, with a general solemn rehearsal of the said commandments, and of all the articles of their faith ... What can be more apt to be grown or painted in the tender hearts of youth than God's holy word? ... What can better keep and stay them, that they do not suddenly and lightly fall again from their faith? What can cause them more constantly to withstand the assaults of the devil, the world, and the flesh, and manfully to bear the cross of Christ, than to learn in their youth to practise the same?[39]

He had now accepted the Bohemian understanding of confirmation. It was 'an ancient and laudable ceremony' consisting of 'an exact and strait examination' of persons of full age as to their understanding of their baptismal faith', after which the bishop or other minister invoked the Holy Spirit to give strength, constancy and other gifts. The efficacy of this latter part, which alone could claim continuity with the historic rite, was the efficacy of the bishop's prayers, but the efficacy of the examination which now constituted the essence of the ceremony depended on that previous instruction in God's word which alone was ordained in the scriptures. It was the word which bestowed strength against temptation, and it was instruction in the word which was essential. Catechisms were an aid to it, and confirmation a guarantee of it.

---

[39] *Ep* cclxxxiv to Edward VI in *Miscellaneous Writings and Letters*, pp. 418–20.

The 1549 baptism service ended with the usual presbyteral anointing, but without chrism and accompanied by a new formula which referred to the unction of the Holy Spirit. Some writers have interpreted this as indicating 'Cranmer's deliberate introduction of Confirmation by a presbyter within the Baptism action itself'.[40] This is surely going too far, but D. R. Holeton and others have seen it more subtly as indicating that Cranmer 'intended to take the entire theological content of medieval baptism and confirmation and place it in his reformed baptismal rite'.[41] This too may be going too far, though it is hard to disagree with it.[42]

A rubric at the end of the baptism service ordered the minister 'that the children be brought to the Bishop to be confirmed of him, so soon as they can say in their vulgar tongue the articles of the faith, the Lord's Prayer, and the ten commandments, and be further instructed in the Catechism'. Taken literally 'so soon as' could imply confirmation at 7 onwards, though the later reference to 'years of discretion' would suggest an older age.

'Confirmation wherein is contained a Catechism for Children' was printed immediately after the baptism service. The introductory rubric explained that for 'the more edifying of such as shall receive it' (a moderate phrase), 'it is thought good that none hereafter' (a pointer to the innovation)

---

[40] E.g. D. B. Stevick, *Baptismal Moments: Baptismal Meanings* (Church Publishing Inc., New York, 1987), p. 20.

[41] 'Christian Initiation: An Ongoing Agenda for Anglicans' in D. R. Holeton (ed.), *Growing in Newness of Life: Christian Initiation in Anglicanism Today, Papers from the Fourth International Anglican Liturgical Consultation, Toronto, 1991,* (Anglican Book Centre, Toronto, 1993), p. 25.

[42] For earlier writers on this anointing, cf. Hamon L'Estrange, *The Alliance of Divine Offices*, LACT (John Henry Parker, Oxford, 1846), pp. 368–70 and 406f, and Charles Wheatly, *A Rational Illustration of the Book of Common Prayer*, vii.2.3 and vii.3.6 (Oxford University Press, Oxford, 1846), pp. 291f. and 394–06. For later writers, cf. also Fisher RP, p. 94, n. 5; L. L. Mitchell, *Baptismal Anointing* (SPCK, London, 1966), p. 179, Marion J. Hatchett, 'The Rite of "Confirmation" in the Book of Common Prayer and in *Authorized Services 1973*' in *Anglican Theological Review* 56 (1974), pp. 292–310.

shall be confirmed, but such as can say in their mother tongue, the articles of the faith, the Lord's prayer and the ten commandments: and can also answer to such questions of this short Catechism as the Bishop (or such as he shall appoint) shall in his discretion appose them in.

Three reasons, derived partly from Hermann's *Consultation* and partly from a misunderstanding of canon law, were given for this. First,

> that when children come to years of discretion and have learned what their Godfathers and Godmothers promised for them in Baptism, they may then themselves with their own mouth and with their own consent, openly before the church, ratify and confess the same, and also promise that by the grace of God they will evermore endeavour themselves faithfully to observe and keep such things, as they by their own mouth and confession have assented unto.

Secondly that confirmation was ministered for strength against temptation and was 'most meet' when children come to that age when 'partly by the frailty of their own flesh, partly by the assaults of the world and the devil, they begin to be in danger to fall into sin'. Thirdly

> that it is agreeable with the usage of the church in times past, whereby it was ordained that confirmation should be ministered to them that were of perfect age, that they being instructed in Christ's religion, should openly profess their own faith, and promise to be obedient unto the will of God.[43]

---

[43] This claim rests on the reference by the 1536 Council of Cologne to the alleged canon of the pseudo-Council of Orleans of 511. But Fisher RP, p. 185, n. 3 (cf. also p. 140) states that '[w]hatever its real source, this canon has been misinterpreted here, because it did not intend that all confirmation candidates must be of perfect age, but that candidates who were of perfect age must make their confession before their confirmation'.

The catechism which followed was defined as 'An Instruction to be learned of every child, before he be brought to be confirmed of the bishop'. It is sometimes claimed that, despite the reference to the candidates ratifying and confessing what their godparents promised in baptism, the renewal of the baptismal vows was introduced only in 1662.[44] But Cranmer was far too skilled a liturgist to make such an elementary mistake as that. The very presentation of the text in which catechism and confirmation are contained in the one order makes it clear, as do the rubrics, that the public examination in the catechism was an examination of faith as well as of knowledge and was itself a ratification of the promises. The child listed what his godparents had promised in his name, and when he agreed that he was 'bound to believe, and to do as they have promised' he was actually ratifying those promises. Similarly when he recited the creed he was not merely attesting his knowledge but also declaring his assent and commitment. As F. W. Puller wrote perceptively,

> Our own Church has provided that her children shall renew their vows every time that they say their Catechism, when they profess that they are bound to believe and to do as their sponsors have promised for them, and that by God's help so they will. Thus our little ones are taught to renew their vows privately whenever they say their Catechism at home, and publicly whenever they are solemnly catechized in church.[45]

The 1971 Ely report also discerned Cranmer's mind rightly when it stated that '[t]he new emphasis on the educational aspect of Confirmation is very clearly brought out in the inclusion of the Catechism within the

---

[44] Cf., e.g. A. C. A. Hall, *Confirmation* (Longmans, Green & Co, London, 1900), p. 6.

[45] F. W. Puller, *What is the Distinctive Grace of Confirmation?* (Rivingtons, London, 1880), p.10. Bucer in his 1551 *Censura, ed. cit.*, pp. 100–7 misunderstood Cranmer when he complained that a mere recitation of the words was required.

pre-1662 Confirmation rites; indeed, in the early Prayer Books the form in which the candidates ratify their baptismal faith is by the replies which they make to the bishop's questions'.[46]

The actual confirmation was *prima facie* not dissimilar to Sarum, and though the laying on of the hand was restored and chrism was abandoned the signing *in fronte* was retained. At the end of the service the first rubric ordered curates, at least every six weeks, to instruct children on some part of the catechism before Evensong, and further ordered parents and masters to cause 'their children, servants and prentices (which are not yet confirmed)' to come to the church at the time appointed,[47] the second ordered them to inform the bishop of the children's names and knowledge, and the third, 'And there shall none be admitted to the holy communion: until such time as he be confirmed',[48] was a shorter and more absolute version of Peckham's ruling. The retention of this has been described as 'an accident' or attributed to 'a certain absence of logic'.[49] But these were not the normal marks of Cranmer's work, and the old rubric now served a new end. There was no exception for the dying because faith not the viaticum was their real need,[50] and there was no exception in cases of 'reasonable impediment', because instruction and examination constituted a *sine qua non*. Had the rubric read, as was its real import, 'And there shall none be admitted to the holy communion

---

[46] *Christian Initiation: Birth and Growth in the Christian Society* (Central Board of Finance of the Church of England, London, 1971) p. 11.

[47] This was a subject of enquiry in the 1550 visitation articles of Nicholas Ridley for London, cf. no. 55, Frere and Kennedy, *op. cit.*, ii.239, and his 1550 Injunctions no. 9, *ibid.*, ii.244. In 1551 Bulkeley included the same article for Bangor, cf. no. 32, *ibid.*, ii.265.

[48] This too featured in Ridley's 1550 articles when he enquired whether clergy admitted any 'before he be confirmed' or 'that ken not the *Pater Noster*, the Articles of the Faith, and Ten Commandments in English'; art. 42, *ibid.*, ii.237.

[49] Cf. G. Dix, *The Theology of Confirmation in Relation to Baptism* (Dacre Press, Westminster, 1946), p. 39, and *Baptism and Confirmation Today* (SPCK, London, 1955), Minority Report, p. 18.

[50] In the 1549 Communion of the Sick, Augustine's 'Believe, and thou hast eaten', repeated in Sarum to those unable to communicate (cf. *Manuale Sarum, ed. cit.*, p. 110), was considerably expanded.

until such time as he be thoroughly instructed and examined in the catechism', the responsibility would have rested with parish priests whose zeal was often uncertain, but by making confirmation the prerequisite Cranmer vested the ultimate responsibility in the bishops, all of whom, if things progressed as he hoped, he would soon be able to trust in the essential matter of examining or appointing suitable deputies. The role of presiding examiner was ultimately the crucial one, just as the examination was the crucial part of confirmation. The imposition of hands which concluded the process was an 'ancient and laudable ceremony' but no more. Far from lacking logic, Cranmer's scheme was a masterpiece of logic. While making few though significant alterations to the medieval rite, he constructed a new scheme for admission which perfectly expressed his own position: baptism, instruction, ministerial approbation, optional confession (which was never actually mentioned in connection with 'first' communion but remained a theoretical possibility), public examination, public profession, laying on of hands with prayer and possibly further instruction.

Sarum had deemed confirmation a prerequisite for admission to communion but not an automatic entitlement to it, and this was probably still the case now even though it was preceded by instruction and examination. Tyndale, regarding the one as a qualification for the other, had suggested 11 or 12 as the age for both confirmation and communion but, unlike Bucer, Cranmer did not envisage confirmation being administered in the context of communion or immediately before a 'first communion' ceremony, and significantly the catechism contained no teaching about communion.[51] It is unlikely that he would have envisaged as lengthy a gap as that advocated by Erasmus, but it may well be that

---

[51] The absence of teaching on communion has traditionally been explained by the suggestion that at this point Cranmer's theology of the sacrament was too uncertain, but the uncertainties did not preclude him from issuing a new liturgy in 1549, and the more one ponders this explanation the less likely it seems.

he envisaged further instruction before admission to communion and the rubric requiring that intending communicants should give advance notice to the curate clearly applied to 'first communion' as to subsequent communions.

Bucer was not wholly satisfied with 1549, and his *Censura* emphasized that it was not enough for children merely to recite words; their confession should be accompanied by such signs in their life as proceeded 'from a heart which truly believes the gospel and from the teaching of the Holy Spirit'. If they showed no such signs, or only modest signs, they would be better left among the catechumens to receive further instruction, for if those only were admitted in whom 'some vigour of the new birth' was manifest, the slower ones, 'if indeed they are born of God', would be excited by their example to make a more serious effort. Moreover, the procedures for catechizing were inadequate. The catechism should be taught on every festal day, not merely one Sunday out of six, and all adolescents, including the confirmed, should attend 'until they have advanced in Christian knowledge to the point when the pastor himself excuses them'. But the restriction of communion to the confirmed 'will be very wholesome if only those are confirmed who have confirmed the confession of their mouth with a manner of life consistent with it and from whose conduct it can be discerned that they make profession of their own faith and not another's'.[52]

Few of these comments could be incorporated in a liturgical text, but in 1552 much that was implicit in 1549 was made explicit. The postbaptismal anointing was omitted and replaced by a post-baptismal signing based on the pre-baptismal 1549 signing, which again associated with baptism the ideas of confession and combat, which had gathered round medieval confirmation and which in its wording, 'We ... do sign him with the sign of the cross" closely resembled the medieval formula at

---

[52] *Ed. cit.*, pp. 100–14.

confirmation, 'I sign you N with the sign of the cross'.[53] Catechizing, as suggested by Bucer and already demanded by Hooper,[54] was ordered not just once in six weeks but on all Sundays and holy days. The requirement that candidates should 'ratify and confess' their vows was amended to 'ratify and confirm', and this was almost certainly deliberate.[55] The bishop still confirmed — 'and the bishop shall confirm them' — but now the candidates also confirmed, and their role was as active as his. The signing and its accompanying declaratory formula, the last traces of medieval form and matter, were removed, the prayer for the Spirit was amended so that God was now asked not to 'send down' the Spirit but to 'strengthen' with the Spirit, and the laying on of hands was accompanied by a new prayer based on Hermann, 'Defend, O Lord ...'. Lastly, the final rubric was altered to read, 'And there shall none be admitted to the Holy Communion, until such time as he can say the Catechism and be confirmed'. At one level medieval confirmation was now firmly rejected in favour of the 'exact and strait examination' of the 'ancient and laudable ceremony', yet Cranmer still retained the laying on of hands with prayer for the Spirit who was invoked in each of the three prayers — 'strengthen', 'increase' and 'be with' — and the rite itself (as opposed to Cranmer's personal theology) was still patent of some kind of traditional understanding.

The interpretation of Cranmerian confirmation offered above is now

---

[53] Cf. the writers mentioned in n. 42 above. For a criticism of their emphasis, cf. the judicious comment of Gordon P. Jeanes, *Signs of God's Promise* (T&T Clark, London, 2008), pp. 280f..

[54] Cf. his 1551 visitation articles for Gloucester, no. 31, in Frere and Kennedy, *op. cit.*, ii.274.

[55] Against this view, an anonymous writer in 'Confirmation' in *Church Quarterly Review* XI (1880), p. 179, suggested that it 'most probably was originally a misprint'; cf. also G. C. Richards, 'Confirmation', *Theology* XLIII (1941), p. 148. J. H. Blunt, *The Annotated Book of Common Prayer* (Longmans, Green & Co., London, 1907), p. 411, thought it was introduced 'out of pure love for a synonym' and compared it with the Declaration prefixed to the Articles in 1628, 'The articles ... which we do therefore ratify and confirm' (no. xci. in Gee and Hardy, *op. cit.*, p. 519).

generally accepted.[56] But many writers in the first half of the twentieth-century misinterpreted Cranmer. Ollard,[57] Michael Ramsey[58] and the 1948 report, *The Theology of Christian Initiation*[59] concluded from 1552's reference to strengthening that he still held the medieval view of confirmation. Others, reflecting the new emphasis on 'Christian initiation' also misunderstood him. Dix praised the reformers' instinct which, 'while allowing infant baptism, made room for the element of conscious faith and response in initiation by postponing Confirmation'.[60] But while the reformers indeed emphasized 'conscious faith and response', they did not see confirmation as part of initiation, nor did they 'make room' for these since the medievals had already done this by requiring confession before communion. *The Theology of Christian Initiation* stated that by insisting on instruction and examination before confirmation, the reformers 'perhaps unconsciously, re-established an important element in the primitive rite of initiation', but it was misleading in its claim that Cranmer brought out the connection between baptism and confirmation as 'two parts of the Christian's initiation'.[61] No reformer suggested that catechizing or confirmation was initiatory, and it is hard to see what important element they 're-established'. Lampe saw as one of their great achievements 'the relating of confirmation to infant baptism in such a way as to make it the means of supplying the response of faith which is required in baptism but cannot be made in the case of infants'. Through public profession of faith the candidate was 'completing his Baptism by the addition to it of what had been an essential part of the adult baptism

---

[56] Cf. R. H. Fuller, 'Baptism and Confirmation', *Theology*, XLIX (1946), pp. 115f, C. O. Buchanan, 'An Anglican Evangelical looks at Sacramental Initiation' in *Faith and Unity* XII (1968) p..47; Fisher RP, p. 243; M. Jackson, 'The Reformation Understanding' in *Communion before Confirmation?* (CIO, London, 1985), pp. 61–76.
[57] Pp. 80–3.
[58] 'The Doctrine of Confirmation' in *Theology* XLVIII (1945), p. 194.
[59] P. 16.
[60] Dix, *op. cit.*, pp. 28–33.
[61] Pp. 12, 16f..

of the early church'. The reformers' development of confirmation 'made it possible to retain infant baptism along with the doctrine of justification *sola fide*', and by demanding profession after instruction they were 'supplying the deficiency which infant baptism would otherwise suffer'.[62] But the reformers would have been embarrassed by much of this praise. *Pace* Lampe, they did not see the response of faith as lacking in the case of infants. It might be supplied by the Word, the Spirit, the parents, the sponsors or the church, but it was not lacking. Nor did they regard infant baptism as either incomplete or partial. As Buchanan rightly says of 1552, 'Confirmation is now clearly seen, within the text of the service as well as in popular belief, as a stage *within* the Christian life, not as an entry upon it.'[63]

In 1553 a new canon law, *Reformatio Legum Ecclesiasticarum*, was presented to Parliament (though never formally approved). This stated that 'We do not want anyone to be admitted to the Lord's Table until he has professed his faith in the Church',[64] and explained that

> To our bishops we give the task to confirm those who have learned the catechism, which must be done particularly in these our times, in which infants who are baptized cannot as yet express their faith and assent. Therefore the time of their confirmation shall be the one most appropriate time for that.[65]

It also sought to strengthen the requirement of signification so that intending communicants were bidden to come together before the minis-

---

[62] G. W. H. Lampe, *The Seal of the Spirit: A Study in the Doctrine of Confirmation in the New Testament and the Fathers* (SPCK, London, second edn 1967), pp. 313f..

[63] *Anglican Confirmation* (Grove Books, Bramcote, 1986), p. 25.

[64] *De Sacramentis* v, *Qui sint admittendi ad mensam Domini*; in G. Bray, *Tudor Church Reform* (Boydell, Woodbridge, 2000), pp. 230f..

[65] *De Sacramentis* viii, *Quo tempore confirmatio esse debeat*, ibid., pp. 230f..

ter on the previous day 'that he may spend time in examining their consciences and ... test their faith'. None were to be admitted whose faith was not perfect in all respects, and if any were uncertain in faith or wounded in conscience they were to receive consolation and, if necessary absolution.[66]

The Edwardine reformers still retained confirmation, though with an emphasis on confession of faith rather than on the Spirit. But when Edward was succeeded by Mary, even the moderate exiles at Frankfurt (including two future archbishops, Sandys of York and Grindal of Canterbury) abandoned confirmation, which they themselves regarded as indifferent but which the stricter party deemed 'offensive and inconvenient', and they insisted only that the youth be catechized and not 'be admitted to the Communion till they be able to make Profession of the Faith before the whole Congregation'.[67]

8 The Elizabethan Settlement

In 1559, after Mary's death, the 1552 book was restored with only a few amendments. But the vision of frequent if not weekly communion had been lost and Parker's 1566 *Advertisements* had to insist that it be administered at least monthly in cathedrals and colleges,[68] a clear indication that the prayer-book's requirement of weekly administration there was widely ignored. But while people were urged to receive the sacrament as often as it was offered[69] or to 'come oftener',[70] its administration remained rare.

---

[66] *De Divinis Officiis* vii, *De Coena Domini sumenda, ibid.*, pp. 338f.
[67] *Ep* ccclvii, 5 Apr 1555, ET *Original Letters*, ed. H. Robinson, PS, ii.753f; also T. Wood (?), *A Brief Discourse of the Troubles begun at Frankfurt*, ed. E. Arber, 1907, p. 145.
[68] LXXXI, no.3 in Gee and Hardy, *op. cit.*, p. .470.
[69] A. Nowell, *Catechism*, ed. G. E. Corrie, PS, pp. 85–95, ET p. 212, cited Green, p. 555.
[70] 1571 canon 4.9 in Gerald Bray (ed.), *The Anglican Canons 1529-1947* (Boydell, Woodbridge, 1998), p. 189. These canons were passed by the Convocations but did not receive the royal assent.

'Confirmation of children by examining them of their knowledge in the Articles of the Faith, and joining thereto the prayers of the church for them' was upheld in the Second Book of Homilies in 1562,[71] and also by Becon,[72] Jewel,[73] Nowell[74] and Calfhill.[75] Nowell contrasted 'this most profitable and ancient confirmation' with 'another used of late', and Calfhill contrasted Roman confirmation with that 'which in the primitive church was, and in the English church is, used'. This distinction between the two confirmations is important for the understanding of Article 25 in the 39 Articles issued in 1563. It was the Roman form, not the 'ancient' and 'restored' one, which was commonly called a sacrament and was described as 'a corrupt following of the apostles'.

Norton, in the preface to his English translation of Nowell, stated that '[t]he end and purpose of catechism is in good and natural order fitly applied to serve the good use of confirmation by the bishop, at which time the bishop which confirmeth doth not teach, but examine'.[76] But even Cranmerian confirmation was too much for some, and in 1571 Puritans in parliament sought to abolish it.[77]

Despite the prayer book, there was minimal reference now to the possibility of private confession and absolution in the course of preparation, and it was the need for instruction and examination which

---

[71] *Of Common Prayer and Sacraments*, traditionally ascribed to Jewel, in *Certain Sermons and Homilies*, 1874 edn, pp. 376–8.
[72] *The Demands of Holy Scripture, Works*, ed. J. Ayre, PS, iii.618.
[73] *A Treatise of the Sacraments, Works* ed. J. Ayre, PS, ii.1125-28.
[74] *Catechism* p.85–95, ET pp. 207–16.
[75] *Answer to Martiall*, ed. R. Gibbings, PS, pp. 212–27.
[76] *Op. cit.*, p. 109.
[77] J. E. Neale, *Elizabeth I and her Parliaments, 1559–1581* (Jonathan Cape, London, 1953), i.198.

aroused the greatest enthusiasm.[78] Elizabeth's 1559 Visitation Articles enquired whether parishioners were admonished not to presume to receive the Sacrament before they could say the three formularies in English,[79] and her Injunctions ordered that young people in particular should be instructed and diligently examined.[80] The 1561 *Interpretations* ordered 'that children be not admitted to the Communion before the age of 12 or 13 years, of good discretion and well instructed before',[81] and in the same year Young, Archbishop of York, forbade any to be admitted who had not previously been communicants 'except they be thoroughly instructed in the catechism ... and be also confirmed'[82] — a reference to confirmation which was unusual at this time.

In 1562 a group in Convocation devised a scheme whereby

> Every person of age and discretion sufficient to communicate, shall offer himself once a year, upon such days as shall be appointed, to be examined by his parson, vicar or curate, whether he can say by heart the articles of his faith, the ten commandments, and the Lord's prayer; upon pain to be Excommunicate *ipso facto*.

Parsons were to use these occasions 'to give some private, godly admonitions to their parishioners, if they know any faults or negligencies

---

[78] On the catechetical instruction of the young, cf. the 1560 Interrogatories of an Ordinary no. 8, *ibid.*, iii.87f.; John Parkhurst's 1561 Articles for Norwich nos. 1012 and Interrogatories nos. 7, 101, *ibid.*, iii.99–101, 107; Parkhurst's 1569 Articles for Norwich nos. 22, 34, *ibid.*, iii.211, 213; Robert Horne's 1569 Injunctions for Channel Islands no. 4f, *ibid.*, iii.220; Edwin Sandys' 1569 Articles for Worcester no 5, *ibid.*, iii.223f. Parkhurst's 1561 article no 5, *ibid.*, iii.98, also required young people to be examined in the formularies before marriage (since they were ordered to communicate on their wedding-day), and bade parsons to 'suffer none to come to the Holy Communion except they also know the same necessary points of religion'.
[79] No. 12, Frere and Kennedy, *op. cit.*, iii.3.
[80] No. 44, *ibid.*, iii.22.
[81] No. 20, ed. W. M. Kennedy, pp. 32, 41.
[82] No. 4, cited by Ollard, *op. cit.*, p. 87f..

in them', but any who 'under colour hereof, shall practise auricular confession' should be deposed from the ministry. Those who could not say the formularies by heart were not to be admitted, unless 'very aged', and each year the clergy were to inform the archdeacon of all parishioners of 14 and upwards who refused to be examined'.[83] This scheme proved abortive, as did the 1563 Articles for Ecclesiastical Government which sought that every person over 14 should present himself annually to the curate to be examined in the Creed, Lord's Prayer and Ten Commandments.[84]

In 1565 Bentham, Bishop of Coventry and Lichfield, charged his clergy to make presentment of 'all children within their cures being full 7 years of age, and not yet confirmed',[85] but Guest, Bishop of Rochester, in 1565 again referred only to instruction and repeated the order in the *Interpretations* but with the age of admission as 13 or 14.[86] The 1571 canons expected children to be communicants by 14, and ordered the curate to send a yearly return 20 days before Easter of the names of those over 14 who refused to receive the communion and also the names of those who refused to be examined.[87] In the same year Grindal of York[88] and Sandys of London repeated this,[89] while Cox of Ely suggested 12.[90]

To facilitate instruction, many other catechisms were used alongside the prayer-book one, sometimes to simplify it and sometimes to supple-

---

[83] 'General Note of Matters to be moved by the clergy in the next Parliament or Synod' 37–40 in G. Bray (ed.), *Anglican Canons*, p. 735f..
[84] *Ibid.*, p. 760.
[85] Art. 7, Frere and Kennedy, *op. cit.*, iii.163.
[86] Injunction 13, *ibid.*, iii.161; for a knowledge of the formularies before communion cf. also art. 2 and inj. 17, *ibid.*, iii.156, 161.
[87] 4.8, *ed. cit.*, p. 189.
[88] Article no. 16, Injunctions no. 7 and 36 in Frere and Kennedy, *op. cit.*, iii.259f, pp. 276f., 287.
[89] Articles 14 and 16, *ibid.*, iii.306f.
[90] Injunction no 5, *ibid.*, iii.297.

ment it.[91] Those of Ponet[92] and Calvin were both influential, as from 1570 were the various editions of Nowell's work,[93] while the titles of some indicated clearly that they were designed for those desirous of communion — an early example here is Marten Micron's 1560 *Short and faithful instruction ... for ... simple Christians, which intend worthily to receive the holy supper of the Lord*. Catechizing was encouraged at home, at school and at church where it was usually given as the Prayer Book ordered before evening prayer, but as early as 1571 Grindal and Sandys referred it as 'before or at' evening prayer. Such instruction and catechizing clearly enabled intending communicants to examine themselves more perceptively and to avoid the risk of receiving unworthily as well as to be better prepared for any ministerial examination that was required.

All agreed on the necessity of self-examination, but the Puritans in particular stressed the necessity of ministerial examination as well. In 1571 Grindal supported them and stressed that all communicants should not only signify their intention but also be examined.[94] In the 1571 Order of Northampton 'the minister and churchwardens went from house to house a fortnight before the quarterly communion to examine

---

[91] Cf. Ian Green, *The Christian's ABC: Catechisms and Catechizing in England c.1530–1740*, (Clarendon, Oxford, 1996), *passim*.

[92] First published in Latin in 1553, but later translated into English.

[93] Nowell issued three catechisms:

a) *Catechismus, sive prima Institution, Disciplinaque pietatis Christianae*, written c.1560, approved the Convocations in 1563, and published in 1570 with ET in the same year, at the request of Parker and Grindal. It was a long work and borrowed much from Ponet and Calvin.

b) *Christianae Pietaris prima Institutio ad usum scholarum*, an abridgement of (a), also published in 1570 with ET in 1572. It is known as 'the middle catechism'.

c) *Catechismus parvus pueris*, published in 1572 with ET in 1577. This was an enlargement of the Prayer Book catechism, with an expanded section on the duty towards neighbours and a treatment of the two sacraments. It is known as 'the small catechism'.

[94] Article no. 16 and Injunctions nos. 7, 8 and 36 in Frere and Kennedy, *op. cit.*, iii.259f, 276, 287.

parishioners on "the state of their lives",[95] and in the same year there were exclusions of the ignorant at Coldwaltham in Sussex.[96]

But whereas the Prayer Book allowed signifying of intention as late as immediately after Morning Prayer (which may have been reasonable when the original practice was 'the Morning Prayer or Mattins to begin between six and seven, the Second Service or Communion Service not till nine or ten'),[97] there had already developed a tendency for the two services to be run together and Grindal ordered ministers not to pause between Morning Prayer, Litany and Communion, but to say them (or the service appointed when there is no communion) without any intermission.[98] In these circumstances examination would have been almost impossible.

---

[95] C. Haigh, 'Communion and Community: Exclusion from Communion in Post-Reformation England' in *Journal of Ecclesiastical History* 51.4 (October 2000), p. 728.
[96] *Ibid.*, pp. 732f..
[97] Peter Heylyn, *Antidotum Lincolniense*, 1637, sec.3, ch. 10, p. 61.
[98] 'Injunction for the Laity', *Remains*, PS, p. 137.

D

Forbidden Categories

9 Those Lacking in Charity

The Prayer Book requirement of charity was reinforced in the Visitation Articles. Elizabeth's royal articles of 1559 enquired whether parsons 'have received any persons to the Communion being openly known to be out of charity with their neighbours or defamed with any notorious crime, and not reformed',[1] and the prohibition was confirmed in her injunctions.[2] Similar enquiries or prohibitions were made by Parker[3] and an unknown ordinary[4] in 1560, Parkhurst in 1561,[5] Thomas Davies for St Asaph,[6] Grindal[7] and Sandys in 1571.[8] The 1571 canons ordered that if any had offended their brethren the churchwardens were to warn them 'brotherly and friendly' to amend. If they failed to amend, they were to report them to the minister 'that they may be warned more sharply and vehemently'. If this proved unsuccessful, they were to 'be driven from the holy Communion till they be reformed'.[9] This requirement was taken seriously in some quarters as early as 1569.[10]

---

[1] No 16 in Frere, *op. cit.*,, iii.3.
[2] *Ibid.*, no. 21, p. 16.
[3] *Ibid.*, no. 6, pp. 82f..
[4] *Ibid.*, no. 19, p. 89.
[5] *Ibid.*, no. 20, p. 102.
[6] *Ibid.*, no. 17, iii.114.
[7] *Ibid.*, no. 15, p.259, and no. 6, p. 276.
[8] *Ibid.*, no. 13, p. 306.
[9] 5.4, *ed. cit.*, pp. 193f..
[10] C. Haigh, *art. cit.*, pp. 721f..

10 Strangers

The medieval disciplinary system rested on the assumption that priest knew his flock, and strangers were therefore normally forbidden to communicate. The first Canterbury series of statutes, c.1213–14, forbade priests knowingly to admit 'a layman from another parish without permission from his own priest'.[11] The first Salisbury series, c.1217–19, repeated this prohibition,[12] and further prohibitions against strangers came from the first Synod of York c.1241–55,[13] a third series of Salisbury statutes c.1228–56[14] and the second synod of London c.1245–59.[15] The London synod made an exception in the case of a traveller 'so long as he is not excommunicated by name or under an interdict', and a similar concession was offered by Peckham at the 1281 Council of Lambeth, 'Let no one offer holy communion to the parishioner of another priest without his explicit permission. But we do not intend this ordinance to extend to travellers or to bind in case of necessity.[16]

The prayer books said nothing about strangers, but Cranmer accepted the medieval tradition, and in his 1550 articles for Canterbury cathedral he asked, 'Whether any inhabitant within my diocese of Canterbury have been admitted to the Communion within their Church, except such as be of the same church?'.[17] Similarly in his Injunctions he ordered that no one be admitted to Communion at the cathedral 'without the express consent of the parson, vicar, or curate, whether he or she dwelleth, first obtained and had; except wayfaring persons, or necessity doth otherwise require'.[18] The prohibition was weakened in 1559, when a Royal Proclamation reauthorizing communion in both kinds

---

[11] Canon 25, PCii.30. Cf. also Constitutions of an unknown bishop c.1225–30, no 31, PC ii.186.
[12] Canons 19, 45 and 62, PC ii 66, 74 and 80.
[13] Canon 19, PC ii 489.
[14] Canon 10, PC ii.513.
[15] Canon 74, PC ii.649.
[16] Canon 1, PC ii.895.
[17] No..3, Frere and Kennedy, *op. cit.*, ii.246.
[18] No. 6, *ibid.*, ii.252.

directed that, where clergy refused this, parishioners who desired it were to resort 'to some other honest, discreet and learned priest or minister either in the same church or some other'.[19] But this was an exceptional situation. Enquiries were made about non-parishioners, i.e. strangers in the traditional sense, in anonymous articles in 1560,[20] by Parkhurst in 1561,[21] and by Sandys in 1571, when he enquired whether the parson 'hath at any time received any that is not of his own parish to the Holy Communion, and for what cause or consideration he hath done so'.[22] The 1571 canons also bade churchwardens to mark whether any strangers came 'more often and commonly' to their church and, if so, to advice the minister 'lest perhaps he admit them to the Lord's Table amongst others, but shall send them rather to their own curates'.[23]

11 Schismatics

The Elizabethan act of uniformity[24] was explicit about the requirement of attendance at church on Sundays and holydays but, while it did not explicitly order reception of communion, this was required in the Prayer Book which it enjoined, and the 1571 canons referred to people coming to communion 'as by the statutes and ecclesiastical laws of this realm they are bound'.[25] The obligation to communicate soon became an important issue. In 1571 a bill for 'coming to the church and receiving of the communion' was introduced into the Commons and was clearly directed against Roman Catholic recusants. Edward Aglionby protested that compulsory communion was a wrongful forcing of conscience, and

---

[19] H. Gee, *The Elizabethan Prayer Book and Ornaments* (Macmillan, London, 1902), p. 95.
[20] No. 29 in Frere, *op. cit.*, iii.90.
[21] *Ibid.*, no. 31, iii..103.
[22] *Ibid.*, no. 15, p. 306f.
[23] 5.28, *ed. cit.*, p. 195.
[24] Gee and Hardy, *op. cit.*, LXXX, pp. 458–67.
[25] 4.8, *ed. cit.*, p. 189.

it was absurd to compel wicked men when the penalty for unworthy reception was death and damnation. But the Puritans thought otherwise. William Strickland argued that in scripture 'the consciences of men were by the prophet restrained', James Dalton maintained that men's consciences did not touch the lawmakers, and Thomas Norton argued that the touchstone by which to identify recusants must be the receiving of communion. The house concurred, as did the Lords, but the royal assent was refused.[26] Interestingly Aglionby had an ally in Bishop Guest who wrote to William Cecil that, while it was lawful and necessary to drive papists to church, 'to enforce them to receive is utterly unlawful; they judge it to be no communion or no lawful communion, and we ought not to give it them because they can in such a case receive it only to their condemnation'.[27]

---

[26] W. H. Frere, *A History of the English Church in the Reigns of Elizabeth and James* (Macmillan, London, 1904), pp. 159–64; Neale, *op. cit.*, i.191–217.
[27] Frere, *ibid.*, p. 164.

E

The Discipline

12 The Minister's Power to Repel

It had always been agreed that by definition the excommunicate should not be admitted to communion. The first series of Canterbury statutes (c.1213–14) forbade priests knowingly to admit 'anyone excommunicated or under an interdict',[1] the first Salisbury series (c.1217–19) repeated this,[2] and the second Salisbury series (c.1238–44) forbade even in danger of death the communicating of 'those excommunicated by name'.[3] But these statutes referred to those who had been formally excommunicated, and the position of 'notorious offenders' was more complex.

The balance between the priest's duties and the people's rights was a delicate one, and it had traditionally been maintained by the concept of notoriety, the insistence that the unworthiness must be known not only to the priest but to society at large. St Thomas distinguished between secret sinners and notorious ones. Sinners were notorious because the fact was evident or because of the judgement of some ecclesiastical or civil tribunal. To them communion should not be given, but to hidden sinners it should be 'since every Christian, from the fact that he is baptized, is admitted to the Lord's table, and cannot be robbed of his right except for some manifest reason'. A priest who had knowledge of the crime

---

[1] Canon 25, PCii.30. Cf. also Constitutions of an unknown bishop c.1225–30, no. 31, PC, ii.186.
[2] Canons 19, 45 and 62, PC, ii 66, 74 and 80.
[3] Canon 16, PC, ii.372.

could warn the secret sinner privately, or warn all openly, from coming without repentance and reconciliation to the church, but although it was worse for the secret sinner to sin mortally in communicating rather than to suffer the loss of his good name, it was worse for the priest to commit mortal sin by unjustly defaming the secret sinner than that the sinner should commit mortal sin. The priest should not commit mortal sin to keep another out of mortal sin.[4]

Lyndwood adopted a similar position. Discussing Peckham's ruling on the necessity of confirmation and its implication that an unconfirmed person could be repelled, he argued that, if the crime was secret and known to the priest only through the confessional (and in this category he included a person's lack of confirmation if others were ignorant of his position), to avoid scandal the priest should admit him rather than publicly repel him.[5] He argued similarly when discussing Peckham's canon on confession before communion, and gave four reasons for the admission of the secret sinner when communicating publicly rather than privately:

> First, he who inflicts a public penance for a secret sin is a revealer of the confession and a betrayer of his crime.

Secondly, every Christian has the right to receive the eucharist unless he loses it through mortal sin. And when in the eyes of the church it is not known that he has lost this right, he ought not to be denied in the face of the church; otherwise evil priests would be given an opportunity to inflict this punishment of their own accord on whoever they wished.

Thirdly, there is the uncertainty as to the state of the one who receives,

---

[4] *Summa Theologica* iii.80.6, ed. Gilby, LIX.54f.
[5] *Provinciale* i.6.40.

for the wind blows where it lists and a man can suddenly be seized, cleansed from sin, and approach the sacrament by divine inspiration.

And the fourth reason is that there would be scandal if he were denied.[6]

We have noted Elizabethan instances of repulsion as early as 1569, but Nowell urged that pastors should 'receive all indifferently, without choice'. Judas had not been turned away from the Supper, nor should hypocrites now 'as long as their wickedness is secret'. Those 'openly known to be unworthy' could be excluded, but the pastor could not debar people if he alone knew of their unworthiness or if he had only been 'privily informed' of it. He could preach at them in public and threaten them in private, 'but put them back from the communion he may not, unless the lawful examination of the church be first had'.[7] Like most features of the Elizabethan settlement this moderate attitude was soon to be challenged but the nature and development of this challenge, and the responses to it, must be considered on another occasion.

---

[6] *Ibid.*, iii.23.233.
[7] *Catechism, ed. cit.*, pp. 217f, cited Green, *op. cit.*, p. 554.

www.ingramcontent.com/pod-product-compliance
Lightning Source LLC
Chambersburg PA
CBHW071319080526
44587CB00018B/3285